Leather CRAFT

The Beginner's Guide to
Handcrafting Contemporary Bags,
Jewelry, Home Décor, and More

Publisher: Amy Barrett-Daffin
Creative Director: Gailen Runge
Developer: Peg Couch & Co.
Senior Editor: Roxane Cerda
Editor: Katie Weeber
Cover/Book Designer: Michael Douglas
Production Coordinator: Zinnia Heinzmann
Photography Assistant: Gabriel Martinez
Front cover/Lifestyle photography by Jason Masters/photo styling by Lori Wenger
Instructional photography by Amy Glatfelter

Published by Stash Books, an imprint of C&T Publishing, Inc., P.O. Box 1456, Lafayette, CA 94549

Library of Congress Control Number: 2022933873

Printed in the USA

10 9 8 7 6 5 4 3 2

Leather
CRAFT

The Beginner's Guide to
Handcrafting Contemporary Bags,
Jewelry, Home Décor, and More

AMY GLATFELTER

an imprint of C&T Publishing

Contents

7 Introduction
9 About the Author

CHAPTER 1:
Getting Started
12 Beginner's Tool Kit
14 Leather
15 Safety

CHAPTER 2:
Essential Skills
18 #1: Cutting a Straight Line
19 #2: Cutting a Curved Line
20 #3: Punching a Hole
22 #4: Setting a Rivet
24 #5: Setting a Snap
26 #6: Setting a Button Stud
28 #7: Using a Wing Divider
29 #8: Using a Four-Hole Punch
31 #9: How to Cross-Stitch
34 #10: How to Saddle Stitch

CHAPTER 3:
The Projects
38 Artist Roll
44 Beaded Ring
48 Bookmark
52 Bow Clutch
58 Card Holder
62 Coffee Cozy
66 Cord Keeper
70 Fringe Necklace
74 Plant Holder
78 Tassel Accessory Set
84 Terracotta Pot Wrap
88 Triangle Wallet
92 Trinket Tray
96 Vase Wrap
100 Wall Pocket
104 Wrap Bracelet
108 Wristlet

Appendix:
116 Patterns

44

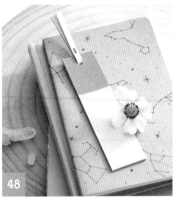
48

52

58

62

66

38

70

74

78

84

88

92

96

100

104

108

INTRODUCTION

Welcome to leathercrafting! I am so glad you have found this book. If you've always wanted to get into leatherwork but felt it was too intimidating, this book is for you. I have a passion for teaching beginners and showing just how accessible leathercraft can be after learning a few essential techniques.

I wrote this book specifically for beginners, hoping that it would attract a new audience of crafters. With the rise of farmhouse style, rustic-chic décor, and all things bohemian, leather is undoubtedly having a moment. I want you to be able to make the projects you love and inject a little bit of luxe leather style into your home and wardrobe.

I designed this book to make your entry into leathercraft as inexpensive and accessible as possible. For that reason, you will notice I have developed projects that can be made from small pieces of leather. Likewise, I have intentionally kept the tools to a minimum. Like any craft, you could go wild investing in beautiful tools that do amazing things, but it's an investment. And, sometimes, you want to try a craft before you spend a bunch of money! So, in the coming pages, I will share my recommendations for a basic beginner's toolset that will allow you to create all of the beautiful projects in this book. Then, as your skills and interest expand, buy more specialized tools. They can be significant time-savers and a joy to use, but let's dip our feet in the leathercraft pond before we get too far ahead of ourselves!

Making things by hand, especially in leather, is fun, but it's also good for you. It can relax your busy mind and be a peaceful respite from the daily grind. I hope you enjoy it as much as I do. And I hope that someday when a friend compliments you on your leather bag, jewelry, or home décor item, you can say, "Thanks, I made it."

XO

Amy

LEATHER CRAFT

About the Author

Amy Glatfelter is a lifelong creative specializing in making heirloom-quality leather goods from her 100-year-old farmhouse and design studio based in Central Pennsylvania. An accidental entrepreneur, Amy started leathercrafting after a cancer diagnosis in 2014. She says, "I was drawn to the tactile aspect of leather and the rhythmic motion of stitching. It helped me relax during long treatment sessions." After years of study, practice, and design development, demand grew for Amy's work, and she launched Arrow Leather Goods. Today, she not only has a thriving leather business but is also a cancer survivor and passionate believer in the healing power of craft. Amy sells her work online and at various art markets and craft festivals. Learn more @arrowleathergoodsusa.

CHAPTER 1:
Getting Started

It is always fun to start a new craft and dive into making beautiful projects. But, taking the time to learn about the essential tools and supplies is very important. This section will review the basic toolset you will need to get started in leathercraft. As I have mentioned before, there's no limit to the wonderful tools you can purchase, but my goal is to provide you with the basics. You'll learn about different kinds of leather (and how to buy it) and the necessary tools such as cutters, punches, and stitching supplies. We will also go over the most crucial aspect of any new endeavor, safety.

Beginner's Tool Kit

Sometimes tools and equipment can intimidate beginners and keep them from starting a new craft. For that reason, I have kept the tools in this book to the bare necessities intentionally. Of course there are many specialty items available for leathercraft, but you can always progress on to them after you've developed your skills and know what investments are best for you. Below is an overview of the tools used in this book.

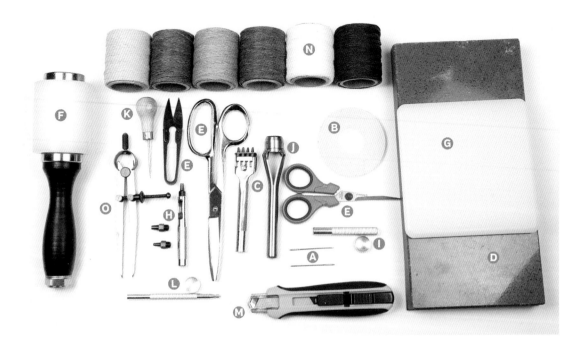

A: Blunt Stitching Needles (Harness Needles)

Stitching leather requires special needles known as blunt-end or harness needles. You will need two of them for cross-stitching and saddle stitching. Do not attempt to stitch leather with standard sewing needles.

B: Double-Sided Tape

It is helpful to baste (or temporarily attach) two parts of leather together before stitching to keep them in place. To accomplish this, double-sided tape comes in very handy. Run a strip of it where you would like to sew and then remove the paper backing, leaving the adhesive behind.

C: Four-Hole Punch

When your leather project requires stitching, you will need to punch stitching holes into the leather. To accomplish this goal, you need a four-hole punch. As the name indicates, it comes with four prongs that will cut holes into leather when you use a mallet to drive them into the material.

D: Granite Slab

A granite slab is a solid surface used under a poly cutting board when you are driving punches, snaps, or rivets into leather.

E: Scissors

Leather scissors (or shears) are specifically designed to cut through the thick material of leather. They are very sharp, so always work slowly and carefully. Protect the blades and do not use them for cutting materials other than leather. In addition to leather scissors, you'll want a pair of craft scissors and thread nippers.

F: Mallet (or Maul)

The vast majority of leather projects involve rivets, snaps, or stitches. Therefore, making holes is essential. To make holes in leather, you will need a punch tool. And to drive the punch tool into the leather, you need a mallet (also known as a maul). It works like a hammer but is specially created to work with leathercraft tools. Never use a metal hammer with metal punches.

G: Poly Cutting Board

This durable cutting board is used over a granite slab to protect your punching tools from damage.

H: Punch Set

Any time rivets, snaps, or stitching are required for a project, you will need to punch holes into the leather. To do so, a punch set comes in very handy. A manual punch set will typically come with a variety of punch sizes to create different hole sizes.

I: Rivet Setter

A rivet setter is used to set a rivet into leather and functions much like the snap setter.

J: Round Punch

As the name implies, a round punch is a punch that is specifically crafted to round the ends of leather. A round punch comes in handy for finishing off bracelets and bag straps.

K: Scratch Awl

Before punching holes into leather, it's good to mark their position. A scratch awl has a sharp tip at the point that allows you to make lines around your patterns and mark holes for cutting.

L: Snap Setter

A snap setter is used to set the parts of a snap into leather. To use a snap setter, place it on the part of the snap you wish to secure and then hit it with a mallet.

M: Utility Knife

Most leathercraft projects start with cutting a small piece of leather from a large one. To make clean cuts, use a utility knife. It is essential to always cut with a sharp blade, so change yours regularly. Avoid the temptation to cut the leather with force. Instead, allow your sharp blade to do the work. When cutting with a utility knife, always use a self-healing cutting mat to protect your work surface.

N: Waxed Thread

Stitched leather projects are joined with waxed thread, which is stiffer and more substantial than standard sewing thread. The common rule to determine the amount of thread needed for cross-stitch is to measure the area to be stitched and multiply it by six. For saddle stitching, multiply the area to be stitched by three.

O: Wing Divider

If you love the look of stitched leather, a wing divider is a must. The tool has two legs with pointed feet. When you run the wing divider against a straight edge, it will draw a straight line that you can follow when punching stitch holes.

> **TIP:** *A quilter's square comes in very handy for leatherwork! Use it to measure, mark, and cut straight lines. I use an Omnigrid quilt square.*

Leather

There is a wide variety of leather available for purchase, but the two kinds we will use in this book are vegetable-tanned leather and chrome-tanned leather. Read the information below to learn more about each kind.

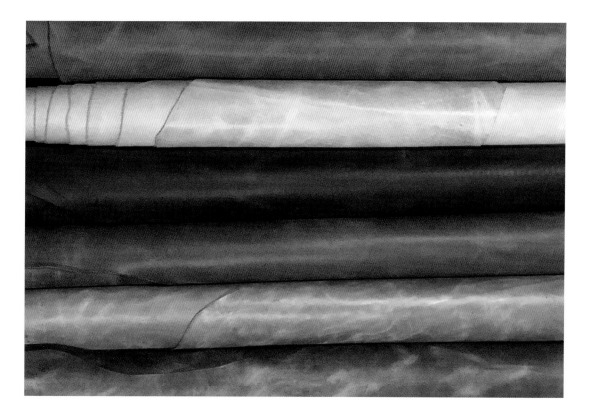

Vegetable-Tanned Leather
This leather is tanned in plant-based materials. It comes in a natural color that can be dyed, painted, and stamped.

Chrome-Tanned Leather
This type of leather is tanned using chromium. It comes pre-colored in many color choices. Chrome-tanned leather is much softer than vegetable-tanned leather and can be used in various projects (including most of the projects in this book.)

Weight and Thickness
When purchasing leather, the thickness is listed in ounces. One ounce is about 1/64″ thick.

Temper
Leather temper refers to the pliability or softness of the leather.

How Leather is Sold
You can purchase leather by the hide or by the side. You can also buy leather by the panel or craft cuts. Many of the projects in this book can be made using smaller craft cuts of leather.

Grain Side and Flesh Side
The grain side of the leather is the outer (or "good") side. The flesh side is the inner side.

Safety

Working with leather requires cutting and punching; therefore, safety is of utmost importance. Here are my top tips for working safely.

1. **Stay sharp.** A sharp blade is a safe blade. Change the blade on your utility knife often. Allow the blade to do the cutting and resist the temptation to force cuts. Always retract the blade and put it away after use.

2. **Cut away from the body.** Always cut in a direction that flows away from the body to avoid accidents.

3. **Work slowly.** Never rush when working with sharp tools. Instead, work slowly to ensure you are working safely. Avoid distractions and focus on your work.

4. **Protect yourself.** Always wear protective eye gear when using punches, mallets, and other tools. A sturdy work apron will protect you from any stray pieces. Finally, do not work with bare feet or sandals; wear protective shoes.

5. **Protective surfaces.** Always use a granite slab under a poly cutting board when punching or using the mallet. Always use a self-healing cutting mat when cutting with the utility knife.

Once you learn the skills in the next section, you will be able to make a variety of leathercraft projects! For example, once you know how to cut leather and set a snap, you can make this gorgeous bracelet!

LEATHER CRAFT

CHAPTER 2:
Essential Skills

Working with leather may seem intimidating, and there are surely many masters of the craft (maybe you will even become one!). But it's also very accessible for the beginner provided that you learn, practice, and master some essential skills. So, in this chapter, I will teach you the foundational techniques you need to make the projects in this book and beyond. We will start with the absolute basics of learning how to cut straight lines and curves safely. Then, we will learn how to set snaps and rivets, which are vital fasteners for leathercraft. And finally—we will learn how to stitch leather so you can give your projects the beautiful, durable, and timeless look that attracted you to this craft. As I will repeat many times in this book, it's essential to work slowly and carefully. Always keep your cutting blades sharp and take breaks when you need them. Now, let's get started!

Cutting a Straight Line

Let's start at the very beginning! Learning how to cut a straight line cleanly and safely is one of the most important skills in leathercrafting. A scrap piece of leather, sharp knife, hard-edge ruler, and a self-healing cutting mat to protect your work surface are all you need.

MATERIALS:

Leather

Ruler

Utility knife

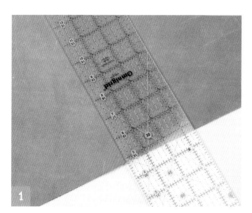

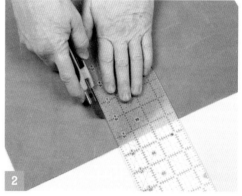

STEP 1: Trace the pattern. Lay the leather down on a flat surface and trace the pattern or cutting line.

STEP 2: Hold firmly and cut. Position the ruler on the cutting line and firmly hold it in place. With your free hand, place the utility knife (blade side down) against the ruler and gently pull it along the ruler's edge to make your cut. Work slowly and safely.

> **TIP:** *If you are cutting thick leather, make several passes with the knife instead of trying to cut through the leather in one pass. A patient leathercrafter is a safe leathercrafter.*

Cutting a Curved Line

Now that you've mastered cutting straight lines, it's time to proceed to cutting curves. Curved lines like rounded corners can add style and sophistication to your projects, but cutting them requires patience and practice. Most of the projects in this book include a pattern to guide your cutting, but you can also use a round object to create a curved pattern.

MATERIALS:

Leather
Scratch awl
Leather scissors (or utility knife)

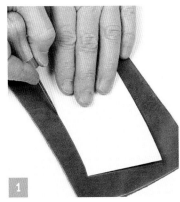

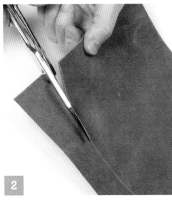

STEP 1: Mark the line and begin cutting. Lay the leather down on a flat surface and trace the pattern or cutting line with a scratch awl. Then, use your leather scissors to start cutting along the line.

STEP 2: Continue cutting to completion. Continue cutting along the line. To ensure a clean cut, work slowly and be sure the blades of your scissors are sharp.

TIP: *If you do not have leather scissors, you can use a utility knife to cut curved lines in leather.*

Punching a Hole

Punching a hole into leather is required when you want to add a snap or rivet to your project. There are various ways to punch holes, but the safest and least expensive way for a beginner to do it is with a basic punch set. As you continue in your leathercrafting hobby, you may wish to add a rotary hole punch or other specialized tools to your collection. Because punching a hole requires striking with a mallet, be sure to protect your work surface with a piece of granite.

MATERIALS:

Leather
Leather punch
Mallet
Poly cutting board
Granite or other protective surface

1

STEP 1: Gather supplies. In addition to your cutting board, leather, mallet, and leather punch, you will need a small piece of granite upon which to work to protect your work surface.

STEP 2: Mark the hole and place the punch. Measure and mark where you would like the hole to be located on the leather. Attach the appropriate punch tip to the punch handle and place it straight up and down with the tip centered on the mark.

STEP 3: Strike the punch. Hit the top of the punch with the mallet. The force will push the tip into the leather to create the hole.

TIP: *Be sure to hold the punch straight while striking to ensure it does not slip.*

STEP 4: Remove the punch. Remove the punch to reveal the hole.

Setting a Rivet

Rivets are used when you wish to join two pieces of leather together permanently with hardware (instead of stitching). Rivets come in a variety of sizes and finishes. For the projects in this book, we will use double cap rivets to give your project a clean finished look. As the name indicates, double cap rivets come with two parts that fasten together, a post and a cap. When selecting rivets, a good rule of thumb is to choose ones that are 2 millimeters longer than your leather is thick. Because this exercise requires using the mallet, be sure to protect your work surface with a piece of granite. (For clear illustration, I do not show the granite in the photos that follow.)

MATERIALS:

Leather
Leather punch
Mallet
Rivet setter and anvil
Double cap rivet
Poly cutting board
Granite or other protective surface

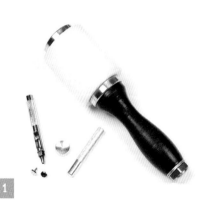

STEP 1: Gather supplies. To practice setting a rivet, you will need a small piece of leather, leather punch, mallet, rivet setter and anvil, double cap rivet, poly cutting board, and something to protect your work surface, like a piece of granite.

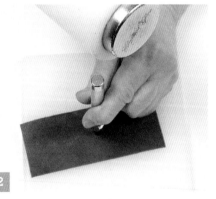

STEP 2: Punch a hole. Follow the steps in Punching a Hole (page 20) to punch a hole in the leather where you want the rivet to go.

STEP 3: Place the post. Push the rivet post through the hole from the flesh side of the leather.

STEP 4: Place the cap. Flip the leather over and push the rivet cap onto the post until you hear a snap. When you hear the snap you will know the pieces are connected.

STEP 5: Prepare the pieces. Place the anvil over the rivet post and lay the pieces flat on your work surface.

STEP 6: Position the setter and strike. Place the rivet setter on top of the rivet cap and strike it with the mallet to secure it.

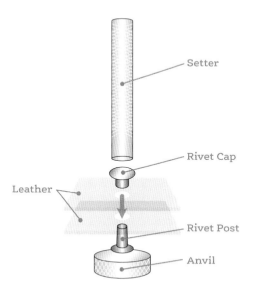

Setter

Rivet Cap

Leather

Rivet Post

Anvil

STEP 7: You've successfully attached your rivet!

Setting a Snap

Snaps come in handy for leathercrafting. You can use them for various projects like bags and small coin purses. A snap has four parts—the cap and socket for the top of the snap and the post and stud for the bottom. A snap is a closure that holds two pieces of leather together, so you will need two pieces of leather for this practice exercise. You will learn to attach the cap and socket of the snap to one leather piece and the post and stud to the other. Because this exercise requires using the mallet, be sure to protect your work surface with a piece of granite. (For clear illustration, I do not show the granite in the photos that follow.)

MATERIALS:

Leather (two pieces)
Leather punch
Mallet
Snap setter and anvil
Snap
Poly cutting board
Granite or other protective surface

STEP 1: Gather supplies. To practice setting a snap, you will need two small leather pieces, a leather punch, mallet, snap setter and anvil, snap, poly cutting board, and something to protect your work surface, like a piece of granite.

STEP 2: Punch the first hole. Follow the steps in Punching a Hole (page 20) to punch a hole in the first piece of leather where you want the snap to go.

STEP 3: Position the cap. Push the cap through the hole from the grain side of the leather.

4

5

6

STEP 4: Position the socket. Put the socket over the cap on the flesh side of the leather.

STEP 5: Strike. Place the anvil flat on your work surface and position the cap on top of it. Place the snap setter on top of the socket and strike it with the mallet to secure it.

STEP 6: Prepare the snap bottom. Follow the steps in Punching a Hole [page 20] to punch a hole in the second piece of leather where you want the snap to go. Push the post through the hole from the grain side of the leather. Put the stud over the post on the flesh side of the leather.

7

STEP 7: Strike. Place the anvil flat on your work surface and position the post on top of it. Place the snap setter on top of the stud and strike it with the mallet to secure it.

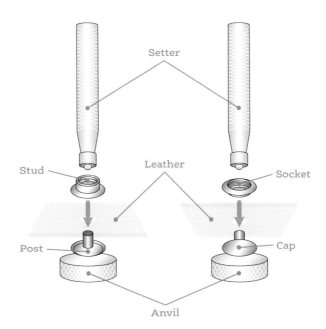

Setter

Stud

Leather

Socket

Post

Cap

Anvil

8

STEP 8: Fasten the snap. Fasten the snap to join the pieces together.

Setting a Button Stud

Button studs hold two leather pieces together and are commonly used for bracelets. In this exercise, I will teach you how to incorporate them into your leather projects. A button stud fits into a hole with a slit. To make holes for button studs, you can use a button hole punch (which makes both the hole and slit simultaneously) or a regular hole punch (and then make the slit with a utility knife). Because this exercise requires using the mallet, be sure to protect your work surface with a piece of granite. (For clear illustration, I do not show the granite in the photos that follow.)

MATERIALS:

Leather strip
Button hole punch (optional)
Leather punch
Mallet
Utility knife (optional)
Button stud
Poly cutting board
Granite or other protective surface

STEP 1: Gather your supplies. You will need a leather strip, button hole punch, leather punch, mallet, button stud, poly cutting board, and something to protect your work surface, like a piece of granite.

STEP 2: Punch the button stud hole. Follow the steps in Punching a Hole (page 20) to punch a hole in the leather where you want the button stud to go.

STEP 3: Insert the post. Push the button stud post through the hole from the flesh side of the leather.

STEP 4: Add the collar and set it. Place the button stud collar on top of the post on the grain side of the leather. Strike the collar with the mallet until the two button stud pieces are joined. To protect your hands, you can place a piece of hard wood over the button stud collar and then strike it with the mallet.

STEP 5: Mark and punch the closure hole. Follow the steps in Punching a Hole (page 20) to punch a hole in the leather with the button hole punch where you want the closure hole to go. If you do not have a button hole punch, make the hole with a regular hole punch, then use a utility knife to cut a small slit extending out from the hole.

STEP 6: Punch additional holes as desired. If you would like, you can make a second closure hole about ½″ (1cm) away from the first one to give yourself sizing options. Now you will be able to secure your bracelet by pushing the button stud through the closure hole.

Using a Wing Divider

A wing divider is an essential tool for the leathercrafter. It has two adjustable legs with pointed tips at the end. It has many uses, but in this book, we will use it to draw straight stitch lines. If you love the look of perfectly straight stitches, you'll want to master this skill.

MATERIALS:

Leather
Ruler
Wing divider

STEP 1: Explore the tool. Familiarize yourself with the wing divider by opening and closing it.

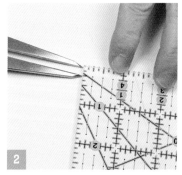

STEP 2: Set the wing divider. Use the ruler to position the legs of the wing divider ¼˝ (0.5cm) apart. Then turn the thumbscrew on the wing divider to lock the legs in place. You can set the wing divider to different measurements, but ¼˝ (0.5cm) is the one we'll use in this book.

STEP 3: Mark a line. Place the wing divider with one leg against the edge of a piece of leather and the other leg on top of the leather. Pull the wing divider toward you, putting pressure on the leg that is on top of the leather. This will make a straight line on the leather. Be careful not to press too hard, or you will mar the leather!

Using a Four-Hole Punch

A four-hole punch is another essential tool for making stitched leather projects. As the name implies, the four-hole punch will create four stitching holes at one time. This exercise will show you how to use the four-hole punch to make a perfectly straight line of stitch holes. You will also learn how to adapt the tool to make elegantly curved stitch hole lines. Always hold your tool straight and use a cutting board on a solid surface like a granite slab to protect your work surface.

MATERIALS:

Leather
Four-hole leather punch
Mallet
Ruler
Wing divider
Poly cutting board
Granite or other protective surface

STEP 1: Mark the stitch line. Follow the steps in Using a Wing Divider (page 28) to set the wing divider to the appropriate width and mark the stitch line on the leather. The line will be your guide for punching the stitch holes. The closer you can follow the line when punching, the straighter your stitches will be.

STEP 2: Position the punch. Place the four-hole punch right on the stitch line, holding it straight up and down.

continued on next page.

Using a Four-Hole Punch, *continued*

STEP 3: Make the first punch. Strike the top of the punch with the mallet. After punching, use your hand to hold the leather in place while you gently pull the punch out of it.

STEP 4: Continue punching. Place the first prong of the four-hole punch into the last hole of the row you just punched. Strike the punch to create three new holes. This process is called over-punching, and it will keep your stitch holes even and straight. Now, every time you punch you will make three holes instead of four because one prong of the punch will always be placed in the last hole made.

STEP 5: Complete punching. As you reach the end of the leather, you may find there's not enough room for a full punch. In that case, position the punch so it will make the number of holes you have room for. For example, if you have room for two more holes, position the punch with two prongs in the last two holes punched. This way, the punch will only make two new holes.

Punching Curved Stitch Lines

STEP 1: Remove the screw. To punch curved stitch lines, like in the case of rounded corners, we'll transform the four-hole punch into a two-hole punch. First, open the punch by removing the screw and nut and taking off the panel.

STEP 2: Remove two bits. Remove two bits from the punch. Then replace the panel and secure it with the nut and screw. Your four-hole punch has now become a two-hole punch. Having a punch with fewer prongs will make it easier to punch curved stitch lines.

How to Cross-Stitch

Not only is cross-stitch beautiful, but it's a practical way to join two pieces of leather together end-to-end. Although this stitch is not complicated, you do need to pay careful attention to ensure that your stitches are nice and neat. To make the cross-stitch, you will thread a needle onto each end of a piece of waxed thread and alternate threading it into the stitch holes, kind of like lacing up your shoes. The result is not only practical but also decorative. Let's get stitching!

MATERIALS:

Leather (two pieces)
Four-hole leather punch
Mallet
Ruler

Wing divider
2 blunt-end leather stitching needles
Scissors
Waxed thread

Thread nipper
Poly cutting board
Granite or other protective surface

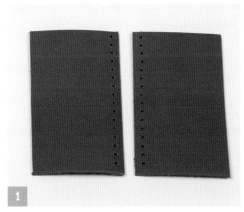

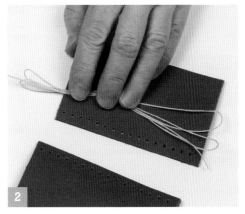

STEP 1: Prepare to stitch. Follow the steps in Using a Wing Divider (page 28) and Using a Four-Hole Punch (page 29) to punch a row of stitch holes along one edge of each leather piece. Place the pieces grain side up on your work surface with the punched edges together.

STEP 2: Determine thread length. Measure the length of the stitch line and multiply by six. Add a few more inches to ensure you don't run out of thread. Then, cut a piece of thread to this length.

continued on next page.

How to Cross-Stitch, *continued*

STEP 3: Thread the needles. Thread a needle with one end of the thread, pulling it through to create a 4″ (10cm) tail. Repeat with the other end of the thread and the remaining needle.

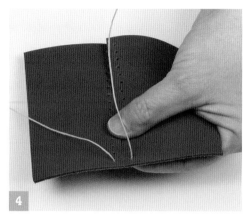

STEP 4: Attach the thread. Working from the flesh side, push each needle through the first hole of each leather piece.

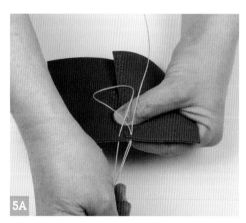

STEP 5: Make a straight stitch. Make a straight stitch by taking each needle and pushing it through the stitch hole directly opposite it. Now the needles will be on the flesh side of the leather. Repeat, pushing each needle through the stitch hole directly opposite it to bring the needles to the grain of the leather.

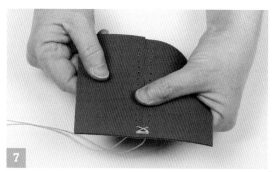

STEP 6: Make the first part of the cross. Take one needle and push it down through the hole diagonally opposite it. Pull the thread taut.

STEP 7: Complete the first cross. Take the second needle and insert it into the hole diagonally opposite it. Now both needles are on the flesh side.

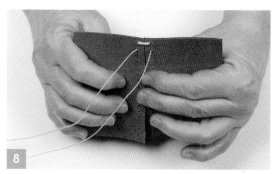

STEP 8: Bring the needles to the grain side. Now the needles are on the flesh side of the leather. To bring the needles back to the grain side, make a straight stitch by threading each needle through the stitch hole directly opposite.

STEP 9: Continue stitching. Repeat Steps 6–8 to make a cross stitch on the grain side of the leather and then a straight stitch on the flesh side. Continue stitching in this manner.

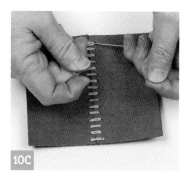

STEP 10: Finish. When you come to the last set of stitch holes, make a straight stitch by threading each needle through the stitch hole directly opposite. Bring the needles to the flesh side of the leather. Remove the needles, tie the ends of the thread in a knot, and trim. For extra security, add a dot of glue to the knot or heat the thread safely with a flame.

How to Saddle Stitch

The saddle stitch is one of the most common stitches in leathercraft and certainly the most durable. Saddle stitches are so durable because they allow you to create two rows of stitches in one row of holes. Many people use a stitching pony to make saddle stitching easier (as it holds the leather and keeps your hands free to work). However, I have intentionally left it out here so that you can keep your initial investment in leathercrafting low. A good tip is to put the leather between your knees to hold it as you work.

MATERIALS:

Leather (two pre-punched pieces)
2 blunt-end leather stitching needles
Thread nipper
Waxed thread

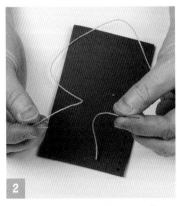

STEP 1: Measure the thread. Measure the length of the stitch line and multiply by three. Add a few more inches to ensure you don't run out of thread. Then, cut a piece of thread to this length.

STEP 2: Thread the needles. Thread a stitching needle onto each end of the thread.

STEP 3: Insert the first needle. Place the leather pieces together with flesh sides facing and the stitch holes aligned. Push one needle through the first stitch hole and pull until there is an even amount of thread on each side.

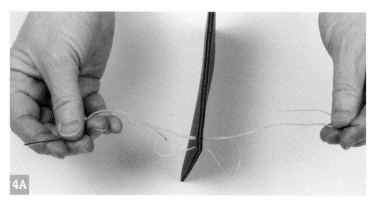
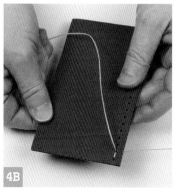

STEP 4: Make the first stitch. Push the left needle through the second stitch hole from the left side. Push the right needle through the second stitch hole from the right side. (Both needles will go through the same hole.) Pull both needles simultaneously to tighten the stitch.

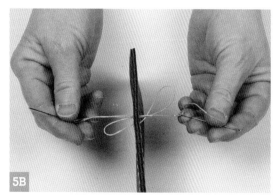

STEP 5: Continue stitching. Repeat Step 4 with the third stitch hole. Continue this process, stitching through each hole to connect the leather pieces.

STEP 6: Backstitch and finish. When you get to the end of the stitch line, saddle stitch backwards (backstitch) through three holes. Trim each end of the thread as close to the leather as you can.

CHAPTER 3:
The
Projects

Now that you have mastered the essential skills for beginning leathercraft, it's time to move on to the fun part! In the coming pages, you will learn how to make a variety of projects. From jewelry and home décor to handbags and wallets, you'll be amazed at what you can create with small pieces of leather, a beginner's toolset, and basic skills. Let's get started!

> **TIP:** *The projects are listed in alphabetical order so they'll be easy to find later. They range in level of difficulty, so find one that matches your skillset to get started. For example, the Fringe Necklace (page 70) and Triangle Wallet (page 88) require no sewing, while the Cord Keeper (page 66) is the perfect project to practice setting snaps.*

LEATHER CRAFT

Artist Roll

We begin our project section with this beautiful artist roll. It is made using several pieces of leather that are joined together with saddle stitching. The project lies flat when the artist is working and needs easy access to colored pencils, paintbrushes, or other materials, then rolls up to store and secure the items conveniently when done. Due to the amount of stitching involved, this is one of the more ambitious projects in the book, so take your time and work patiently. The result is undoubtedly worth the time investment!

Cutting a Straight Line | pg. 18
Punching a Hole | pg. 20
Setting a Rivet | pg. 22
Setting a Snap | pg. 24
Using a Wing Divider | pg. 28
Using a Four-Hole Punch | pg. 29
How to Saddle Stitch | pg. 34

ESSENTIAL SKILLS

MATERIALS

- Leather: 18″ × 24″ (46 × 61cm), soft, 4–5oz
- Medium double-cap rivet
- #20 snap
- Single-hole leather punch with 5/32″ (4mm) tip
- Four-hole leather punch
- Rivet setter and anvil

- Snap setter and anvil
- Mallet
- Utility knife
- Scratch awl
- Ruler
- Poly cutting board
- Wing divider

- 2 blunt-end stitching needles
- Thread nipper
- Waxed thread
- Thin, double-sided tape
- Artist Roll Pattern (pages 116–117)

TIP
This clever design has a built-in flap to protect your art materials. Be sure to tuck the working end of your colored pencils or paintbrushes under it before rolling it up.

Artist Roll

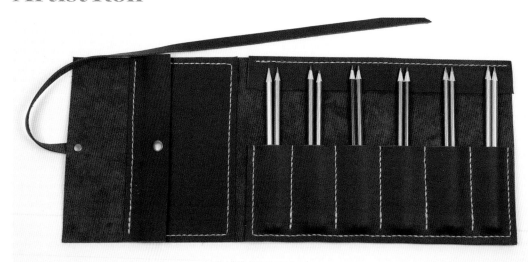

Here is a look at the interior of the project. Please refer to this image as needed while assembling the pattern pieces.

STEP 1: Trace and cut the pattern. Lay the pattern pieces on the leather and trace each one with the scratch awl. Cut out the pieces using the utility knife and ruler.

STEP 2: Tape the pieces. On the flesh side of the leather, add double-sided tape to the edges of the pencil holder, top flap, pocket flap, and pocket as shown in the photo. The tape will hold the pieces in place temporarily while you punch and stitch them to the main body.

STEP 3: Mark the position of the snap holes. Place the pattern pieces for the pocket and pocket flap over their matching leather pieces. Mark the position of the snap holes with the scratch awl.

STEP 4: Set the snap. Set the top of the snap in the pocket flap and the bottom of the snap in the pocket.

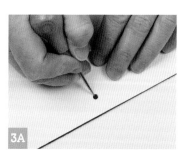

STEP 5: Place the pencil holder and top flap on the body. Place the main body piece flesh side up. Remove the backing from the double-sided tape on the pencil holder and top flap. With flesh sides facing, press the top flap and pencil holder into place on the main body. The top flap should align with the top edge and top right corner of the main body. The pencil holder should align with the bottom edge and bottom right corner.

STEP 6: Mark and place the pocket. Measure and make a mark 3½″ (9cm) in from the left end of the main body (the end without the pencil holder). Remove the backing from the double-sided tape on the pocket. Press the pocket onto the main body with flesh sides facing, placing the edge with the snap at the 3½″ (9cm) mark.

STEP 7: Add the pocket flap. Remove the backing from the double-sided tape on the pocket flap. Use the snap to line it up with the pocket and press it into place on the main body with flesh sides facing. Close the snap for extra security.

STEP 8: Mark the stitch lines. Set the wing divider to ¼″ (0.5cm) and mark the stitch lines on the pocket, pocket flap, top flap, and the edges of the pencil holder. Refer to the pattern as needed.

Artist Roll

STEP 9: Plot the pencil holder stitch lines.
Use the pattern piece and the scratch awl to mark guidelines along the top and bottom edges of the pencil holder showing where the pocket stitch lines will go.

STEP 10: Mark the pencil divider stitch lines. Use the wing divider and ruler to mark the pocket stitch lines by connecting the guidelines marked at the top edge of the pencil holder with the corresponding guidelines marked at the bottom edge.

STEP 11: Punch the stitch lines. Use the four-hole punch to punch the stitch lines. To keep your punch lines straight, remember to over-punch. Work slowly and carefully as there are many holes to punch on this project.

STEP 12: Punch the strap hole on the body.
Use the pattern piece and the scratch awl to mark the position of the rivet hole on the main body. Punch the hole.

STEP 13: Make the strap. Use the ruler and utility knife to cut a 24″ × ½″ (61 × 1cm) piece of leather for the strap. Punch a hole at one end of the strap.

STEP 14: Set the strap rivet. Place the main body grain side up. Place the strap grain side up on the end opposite the pencil holder, lining up the holes for the rivet. Attach the strap to the main body using a rivet.

STEP 15: Stitch the top flap. Measure the top flap's stitch line and multiply by three to determine the length of thread you need. Cut the thread to length and thread a needle onto each end. Saddle stitch the top flap to the main body.

STEP 16: Stich the pencil holder. Follow the same process to saddle stitch the edges of the pencil holder to the main body.

STEP 17: Stitch the pencil holder pocket dividers. Follow the same process to saddle stitch the pocket dividers for the pencil holder.

STEP 18: Stitch the pocket and flap. Follow the same process to saddle stitch the pocket and pocket flap to the main body.

STEP 19: Fill and roll. Your project is complete! Fill it with your favorite art instruments, roll it up, and secure it with the strap.

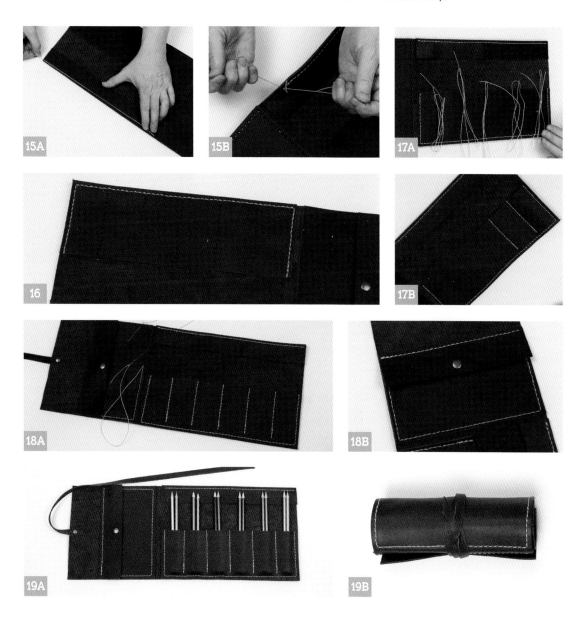

LEATHER CRAFT

Beaded Ring

Dress it up or dress it down! This gorgeous leather ring is the epitome of understated elegance. I love how the rustic texture of the leather complements the smooth freshwater pearl. It is a ring that would look just as beautiful with your favorite jeans or a cashmere sweater! The project goes together quickly with no stitching, but it does require a little patience as we are working on a small scale. No pattern is needed for this project, as I will teach you how to size the ring to fit your finger perfectly. Make a few and try different beads to change up the look.

Cutting a Straight Line | pg. 18
Punching a Hole | pg. 20

ESSENTIAL SKILLS

MATERIALS

- Leather: 1″ × 5″ (2.5 × 12.5cm), soft, 3oz
- 2mm leather cord
- Pre-drilled freshwater pearl or another bead
- Single-hole leather punch with ³⁄₃₂″ (2.5mm) tip
- Mallet
- Utility knife
- Scratch awl
- Ruler
- Poly cutting board

TIP
This ring will stretch a little with wear so it's okay if it is a bit snug on your finger at first. Also, remember to remove your ring whenever washing or working in water.

Beaded Ring

STEP 1: Cut a strip of leather. Use the utility knife and ruler to cut a 4″ × ½″ (10 × 1cm) strip of leather.

STEP 2: Fit to finger. Wrap the leather strip around the finger upon which you will wear the ring to gauge its approximate size.

STEP 3: Adjust and mark the measurement. When sizing the ring, we need to account for the pearl. Note the length of the leather strip sized to your finger. Now subtract the width of the pearl. Use the scratch awl to mark this measurement on the leather strip.

STEP 4: Cut to size. Cut the leather strip to the size measured in Step 3 (the fit around your finger minus the width of the pearl).

STEP 5: Punch two holes. Punch a hole at each end of the leather strip, about ⅛″ (0.5cm) in from the edge.

STEP 6: Assemble the ring. Thread the cord through one of the holes in the leather strip from the grain side. String the pearl onto the cord. Bring the cord through the hole at the other end of the leather strip.

STEP 7: Knot the cord. Pinch the components together tighly and secure them in place by tying a knot in the cord on either side.

STEP 8: Trim the cord. After your knots are complete, trim each end of the cord as close to the knot as possible.

STEP 9: Your ring is complete!

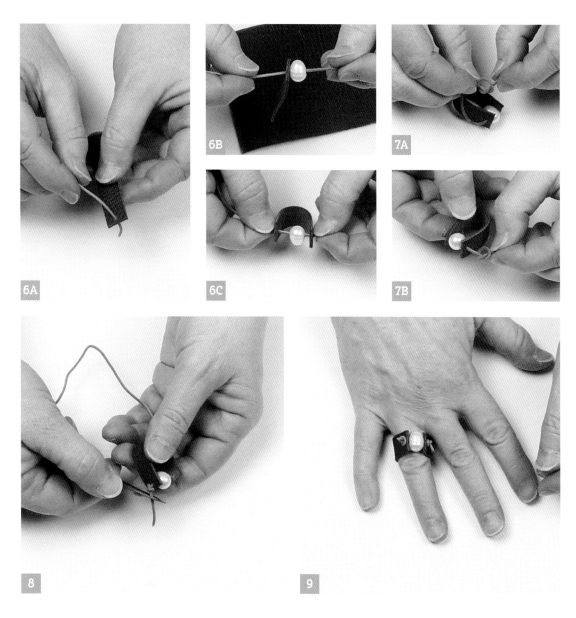

LEATHER CRAFT

Bookmark

I will admit it; I am a giant book nerd! I have loved reading since I was a kid and have very fond memories of ordering books in school. In fact, I still have all of my favorite childhood books in my attic. So, if you're a book lover like me, this project is for you! This bookmark is made from vegetable-tanned leather and finished with a fun pop of pink leather dye. This is a simple project that only requires a few stitches. So, make a bunch and give them as gifts to your favorite reader.

Cutting a Straight Line | pg. 18
Punching a Hole | pg. 20

ESSENTIAL SKILLS

MATERIALS

- Vegetable-tanned leather: 2″ × 6″ (5 × 15cm), firm, 3–4 oz
- Single-hole leather punch with ⁹/₃₂″ (7mm) tip
- Two-hole leather punch
- Mallet
- Utility knife

- Scratch awl
- Ruler
- Poly cutting board
- Blunt-end stitching needle
- Thread nipper

- Waxed thread
- Leather dye and dauber
- Tape (masking or painter's)
- Bookmark Pattern (page 118)

TIP

Try swapping the pink waxed thread for a small rivet to change up the look of this bookmark.

Bookmark

STEP 1: Mark and cut the leather. Trace the pattern onto the leather and mark the position of the holes. Use the ruler and utility knife to cut out the pieces.

STEP 2: Punch the holes. Use the single-hole punch to punch the hole at the top of the bookmark where marked. Use the two-hole punch to punch the holes in the strap where marked.

STEP 3: Tape the paint area. Place a strip of painter's tape across the bookmark approximately 2½˝ (6.5cm) down from the top (the end with the hole).

STEP 4: Paint the top of the bookmark. Dip the dauber into the leather dye and gently brush it onto the area above the tape. Let it dry according to the manufacturer's instructions.

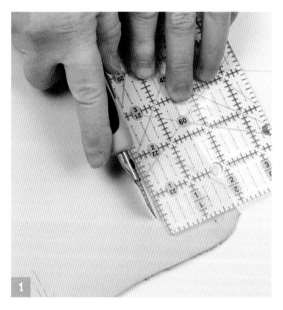

1

2A

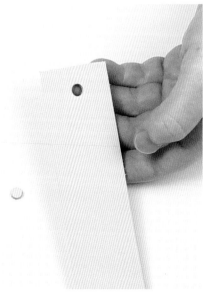

2B

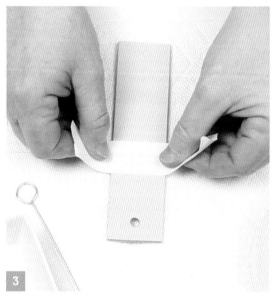

3

STEP 5: Insert strip and thread. Push the thin strip of leather through the hole of the bookmark and pull it until both ends are even and the holes line up. Bring the thread through the lower two holes from the back. Then bring it down through the upper two holes so both ends of the thread are on the back side of the bookmark as shown. Use a needle to help poke the thread through the holes if needed.

STEP 6: Tie the thread. Tie the ends of the thread into a small knot on the back of the bookmark and secure the knot.

STEP 7: Your bookmark is complete!

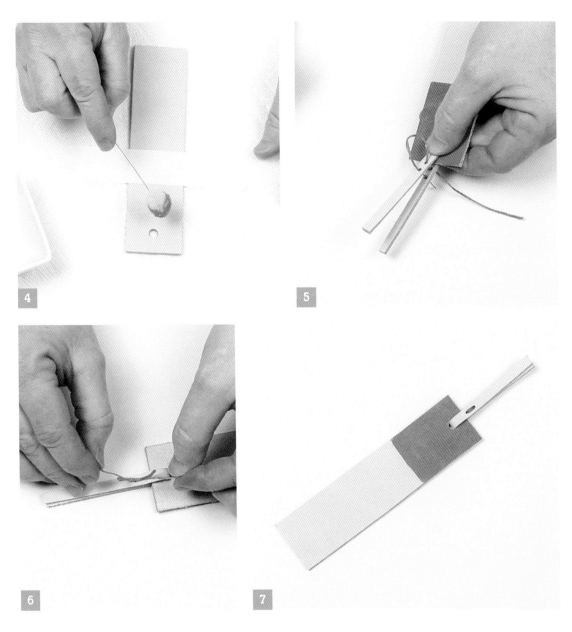

Bow Clutch

This sassy little clutch is the perfect accessory to finish off any outfit. While it may seem intimidating to make at first, it's highly achievable if you follow the instructions. When sewing the sides together, pay special attention to ensure that the holes line up perfectly. Then, you'll have a perfect bag full of personality that will never go out of style!

Cutting a Straight Line | pg. 18
Cutting a Curved Line | pg. 19
Using a Wing Divider | pg. 28
Using a Four-Hole Punch | pg. 29
How to Cross-Stitch | pg. 31
How to Saddle Stitch | pg. 34

ESSENTIAL SKILLS

MATERIALS

- Leather: 15″ × 20″ (38 × 51cm), medium to firm, 5oz
- Four-hole leather punch
- Mallet
- Utility knife
- Scratch awl

- Leather scissors
- Ruler
- Poly cutting board
- Wing divider
- 2 blunt-end stitching needles

- Thread nipper
- Waxed thread
- Bow Clutch Pattern (page 119)

TIP
Set it and forget it! Keep the wing divider set at ¼″ (0.5cm) for all pieces in this project. Your lines will stay even, and the project will fit together perfectly.

Bow Clutch

STEP 1: Trace and cut the pattern. Lay all of the pattern pieces on the leather and trace them with the scratch awl. Be sure to trace two side panels as marked on the pattern. Use the utility knife to cut out the pieces. If desired, use leather scissors to cut around the curved parts.

STEP 2: Mark the stitch line on the body. Set the wing divider to ¼″ (0.5cm). Starting 12″ (30.5cm) from the bottom edge, mark a stitch line on each side of the body.

STEP 3: Punch the body stitch line. Use the four-hole punch to punch the stitch lines on each side of the body. Remember to over-punch to keep your stitch holes straight.

STEP 4: Mark the stitch lines on the hand strap. Set the wing divider to ¼″ (0.5cm) and mark a stitch line at each short end of the hand strap.

STEP 5: Punch the hand strap holes. Use the four-hole punch to punch the stitch holes for the hand strap. You should have room to make eight stitch holes at each end of the strap.

STEP 6: Mark the stitch lines on the bow piece. Set the wing divider to ¼″ (0.5cm) and mark a stitch line at each short end of the bow piece.

STEP 7: Punch the bow piece. Use the four-hole punch to punch the stitch holes for the bow piece. You should have room to make six stitch holes at each end of the piece.

STEP 8: Mark the stitch lines on the side panels. Set the wing divider to ¼″ (0.5cm) and mark a stitch line around the edge of each side panel. Do not mark a line along the base of the panels as they will not be stitched. Refer to the pattern as needed.

STEP 9: Punch the side panel holes. Use the four-hole punch to punch the stitch holes for the side panels. When you reach the curved section, remove two bits from the punch (making it a two-hole punch) and continue punching around the curve. Each side panel should have fifty stitch holes. Refer to the pattern as needed.

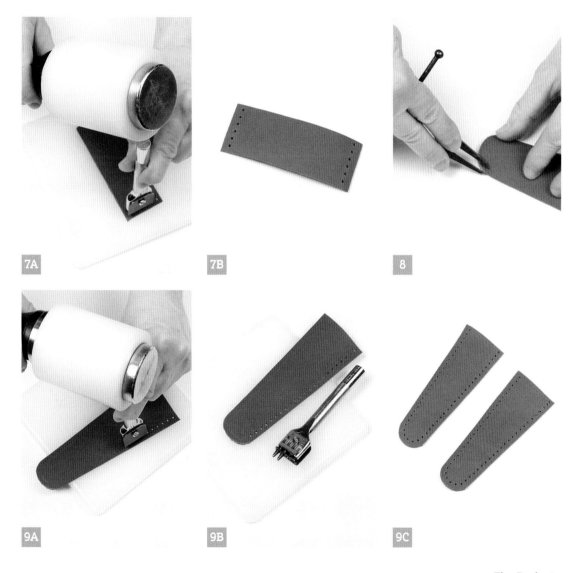

7A

7B

8

9A

9B

9C

Bow Clutch

STEP 10: Stich the bow piece. Lay the bow piece on the work surface (flesh side up) and lay the hand strap across it (also flesh side up). Bring the ends of the bow piece together so the stitch holes are side-by-side. Cross-stitch the ends of the bow piece together.

STEP 11: Attach the first side panel and begin stitching. Align the bottom of a side panel with a bottom corner of the body piece (flesh sides facing). Thread each needle with one end of the thread. Make a stitch around both leather pieces at the corner to connect them. Line up the stitch holes and saddle stitch through six holes.

STEP 12: Attach the handle. Place the body piece grain side up. Place the handle grain side up on top of the body. Line up the first stitch hole on the end of the handle with the seventh stitch hole of the body piece so you have open holes

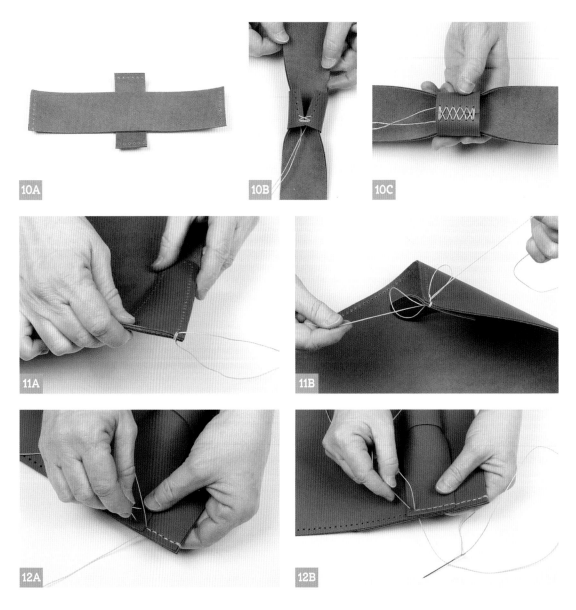

10A

10B

10C

11A

11B

12A

12B

for stitching. Continue saddle stitching through the layers (side panel, body piece, and handle) to attach the handle to the body.

STEP 13: Continue stitching around the side panel. Keep saddle stitching the side panel to the body piece. Slowly fold the body piece around the panel so that the holes meet. You will see the flat pieces form into the bag's shape.

STEP 14: Stitch the other side panel. Repeat Steps 11–13 to stitch the remaining side panel to the other side of the body and secure the other end of the handle. Stitch slowly to ensure that the hand strap and side panel holes line up perfectly with the body piece on both sides.

STEP 15: Tuck and go! Tuck the flap of the bag under the handle to close it.

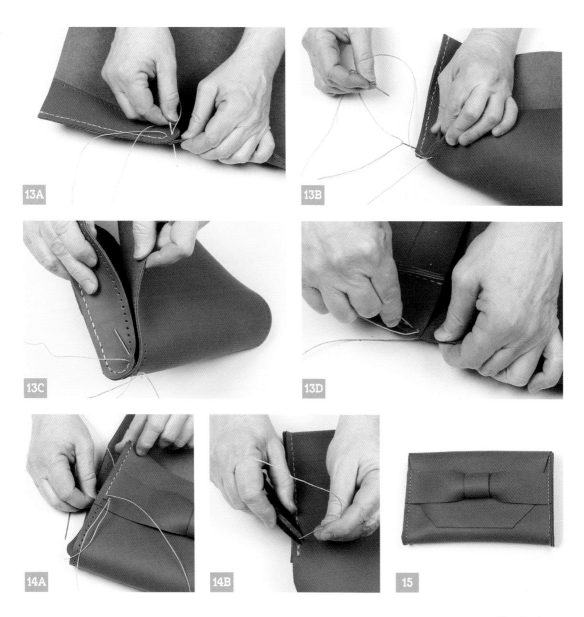

13A

13B

13C

13D

14A

14B

15

Card Holder

Here is a cute little card holder project that comes together quickly. You can use it to store your credit cards, business cards, or even spare change. It's perfect for using up small scraps of leather and makes a beautiful gift. I hope you enjoy making it as much as I do!

Cutting a Straight Line | pg. 18
Punching a Hole | pg. 20
Setting a Snap | pg. 24
Using a Wing Divider | pg. 28
Using a Four-Hole Punch | pg. 29
How to Saddle Stitch | pg. 34

ESSENTIAL SKILLS

MATERIALS

- Leather: 5″ × 8″ (12.5 × 20.5cm), medium, 4oz
- #20 snap
- Single-hole leather punch with $\frac{5}{32}$″ (4mm) tip
- Four-hole leather punch
- Snap setter and anvil

- Mallet
- Utility knife
- Scratch awl
- Ruler
- Poly cutting board
- 2 blunt-end stitching needles

- Thread nipper
- Waxed thread
- Thin, double-sided tape
- Card Holder Pattern (page 120)

TIP
Try enlarging this pattern to make a matching wallet!

Card Holder

STEP 1: Trace the pattern. Lay the pattern on the leather and trace the outline with the scratch awl.

STEP 2: Mark the holes and cut the leather. Use the scratch awl to mark the holes for the snaps on the leather. Use the utility knife to cut out the card holder.

STEP 3: Punch the holes. Punch the holes marked for the snaps.

STEP 4: Set the snap. Set the snap. Be sure to position the pieces so the snap will close when the card holder is assembled.

STEP 5: Tape the sides. On the flesh side of the leather, attach a piece of tape to the card holder going from the bottom edge to about 5″ (12.5cm) up the side. Repeat on the other side. Remove the backing from the tape.

STEP 6: Fold and pinch. Fold the bottom edge of the leather up to the 5″ (12.5cm) line. The flesh sides should be facing. Press the layers together so the fold is held in place by the tape.

STEP 7: Mark the stitch line. Set the wing divider to ¼″ (0.5cm) and use it to draw a stitch line on the short sides of the card holder.

STEP 8: Punch the stitch holes. Use the four-hole punch to punch the stitch lines on each side of the card holder. Remember to over-punch to keep your stitch holes straight.

STEP 9: Prepare the thread. Measure the stitch line on one side of the card holder and multiply by three to determine the length of thread you need. Cut the thread to length and thread a needle onto each end.

STEP 10: Stich the sides. Saddle stitch one side of the card holder, then repeat on the other side. Remember to backstitch through three holes to secure the stitching.

STEP 11: Snip and secure the ends. Use your thread nipper to nip off the ends of the thread.

STEP 12: Your card holder is complete!

7

8A

8B

9

10

11

12

Coffee Cozy

Skip the disposable coffee cozy and make your own! This cute little project is fun to make and sturdy enough to stand up to your daily grind. Simply cut a piece of leather using the pattern found in the back of the book and follow the instructions to make perfect stitches. Life's too short to have boring beverages. So give your favorite hot beverage a sophisticated upgrade with this handmade leather wrap.

Cutting a Straight Line | pg. 18
Cutting a Curved Line | pg. 19
Using a Wing Divider | pg. 28
Using a Four-Hole Punch | pg. 29
How to Saddle Stitch | pg. 34

ESSENTIAL SKILLS

MATERIALS

- Leather: 3″ × 11″ (7.5 × 28cm), medium to firm, 5oz
- Four-hole leather punch
- Mallet
- Utility knife

- Leather scissors
- Scratch awl
- Ruler
- Poly cutting board
- Wing divider

- 2 blunt-end stitching needles
- Thread nipper
- Waxed thread
- Coffee Cozy Pattern (page 121)

TIP
Want to create this project in a different size to match a smaller or larger cup? Simply follow the pattern-making technique in the Pot Wrap project on page 84.

Coffee Cozy

STEP 1: Trace the pattern. Lay the pattern on the leather and trace the outline with the scratch awl.

STEP 2: Cut the ends. Use the utility knife to cut the straight ends of the cozy.

STEP 3: Cut the curved lines. Use leather scissors to cut the curved top and bottom edges. Work slowly to ensure you get clean cuts.

STEP 4: Mark the stitch lines. Set the wing divider to ¼″ [0.5cm] and mark a stitch line at each short end of the cozy.

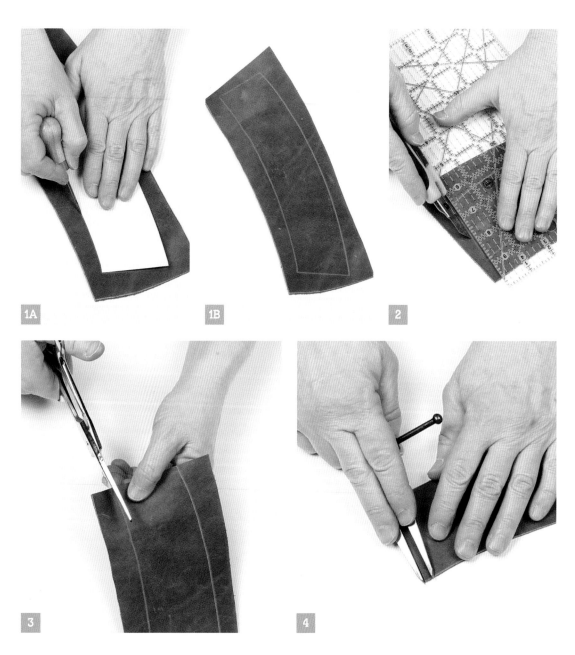

1A

1B

2

3

4

STEP 5: Punch the stitch holes. Use the four-hole punch to punch the stitch lines on each end of the cozy. Remember to over-punch to keep your stitch holes straight.

STEP 6: Join the sides. Bring the ends of the cozy together to align the holes.

STEP 7: Stitch the holes. Saddle stitch the ends of the cozy together.

STEP 8: Secure the stitches. When finished stitching, tie the ends of the thread in a knot and secure it.

5A

5B

6

7

8

Cord Keeper

Oh, the cords, chargers, and batteries. Is it just me, or have electronics overrun your household as well? If you've ever dug to the bottom of your bag to find your earbuds and pulled out a tangled mess (I see you), this project is for you! This is the most straightforward project to make and the most practical. Just cut a circle, set your snap, and organize those crazy cords. You got this!

Cutting a Curved Line | pg. 19
Punching a Hole | pg. 20
Setting a Snap | pg. 24

ESSENTIAL SKILLS

MATERIALS

- Leather: 4˝ × 4˝ (10 × 10cm), soft to medium, 3–4oz
- #20 snap
- Single-hole leather punch with 5/32˝ (4mm) tip
- Snap setter and anvil
- Mallet
- Leather scissors
- Scratch awl
- Poly cutting board
- Cord Keeper Pattern (page 122)

TIP
This is a great first project to practice setting a snap!

Cord Keeper

STEP 1: Place the pattern.
Lay the pattern on the leather.

STEP 2: Trace the pattern.
Trace the outline of the pattern with the scratch awl.

STEP 3: Cut the pattern.
Use leather scissors to cut out the circle carefully. Be sure to work slowly to get a good, clean cut.

STEP 4: Fold and punch.
Fold the circle in half (it should look like a taco) and punch a hole at the top of the curve (see the pattern for placement).

STEP 5: Set the snap.
Set the snap. Be sure to position the pieces so the snap will close.

STEP 6: Your cord keeper is done! Now you can wrap up a cord and place it in the cord keeper for easy organization and storage.

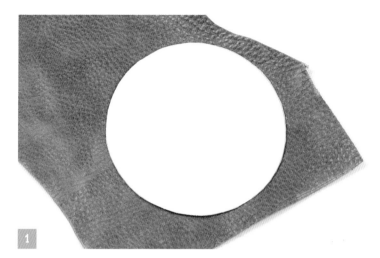

1

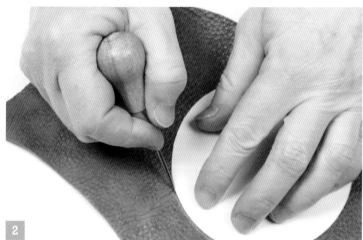

2

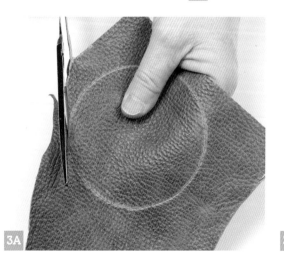

3A

3B

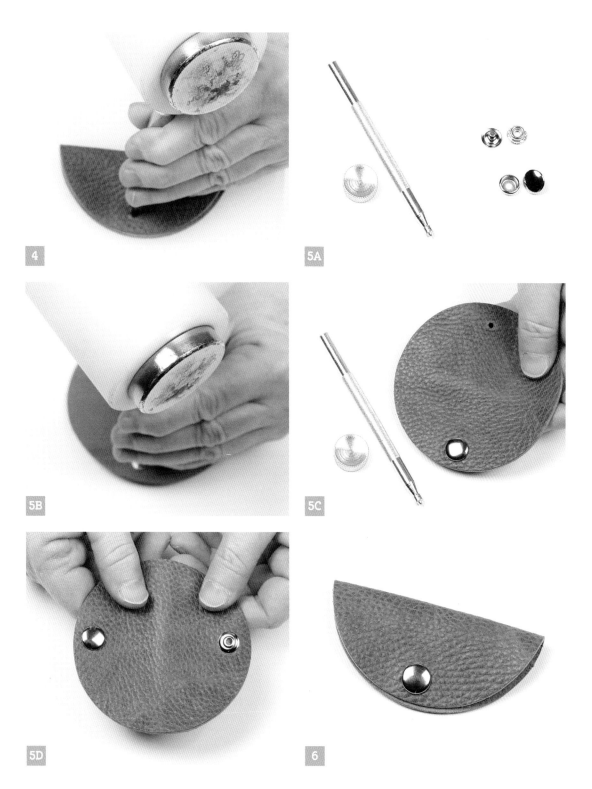

4

5A

5B

5C

5D

6

Fringe Necklace

If you love a good statement necklace, this project is for you. This rustic-chic fringe necklace is defined by eye-catching hardware. It's an excellent project for beginners as no stitching, snaps, or rivets are required. Simply cut the leather to length and follow the instructions to secure it to the ring using a lark's head knot. Then, attach a chain with simple jewelry findings, and voilà, you have an instant accessory that will add boho flair to any outfit.

Cutting a Straight Line | pg. 18

ESSENTIAL SKILLS

MATERIALS

- Leather: 2″ × 3″ (5 × 7.5cm), soft, 2oz
- 24″ (61cm)-long chain in antique brass
- 1″ (2.5cm) O-ring in antique brass
- Utility knife
- Ruler

TIP

Once complete, you can cut the fringe on this project so all pieces are even. Or, you can leave them at different lengths for a more casual and carefree look.

Fringe Necklace

STEP 1: Measure and cut the leather strips. Use the ruler and utility knife to cut out three 3″ × ¼″ (7.5 × 0.5cm) leather strips.

STEP 2: Stack the strips. Stack the strips on top of one another with the grain sides facing up.

STEP 3: Fold and thread. Fold the strips in half to form a loop in the center. Thread the loop through the ring.

STEP 4: Pull through. Grab the ends of the strips, pull them through the loop, and pull tight. This is called a lark's head knot.

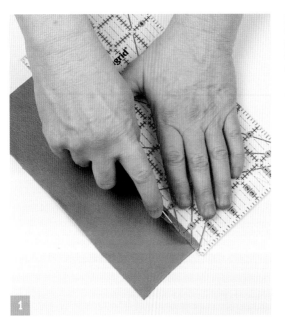

1

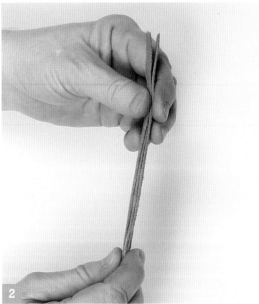

2

3A

3B

STEP 5: Adjust and tighten. Use your fingers to adjust the leather until you have the three pieces at the top of the knot neatly organized. This takes a little time, so work with the leather and have fun.

STEP 6: Finish and enjoy! Add a chain, and you have a cute boho necklace!

4

5A

5B

6

Plant Holder

Dried flowers, faux florals, and air plants are the perfect way to bring some life into your home if you're not blessed with a green thumb. And if you are looking for a unique way to display them, this project is perfect! This cone-shaped leather wall hanger is easy to make and just the right size to showcase a small plant collection. We will practice the cross-stitch in this project, so get your needles ready and let's go!

Cutting a Straight Line | pg. 18
Using a Wing Divider | pg. 28
Using a Four-Hole Punch | pg. 29
How to Cross-Stitch | pg. 31

ESSENTIAL SKILLS

MATERIALS

- Leather: 4″ × 4″ (10 × 10cm), firm, 5oz
- Single-hole leather punch with ⁵⁄₃₂″ (4mm) tip
- Four-hole leather punch
- Mallet
- Utility knife

- Scratch awl
- Ruler
- Triangle ruler (optional)
- Poly cutting board
- Wing divider

- 2 blunt-end stitching needles
- Thread nipper
- Waxed thread
- Plant Holder Pattern (page 118)

TIP

Be sure to remove air plants from the holder before watering.

Plant Holder

STEP 1: Trace the pattern. Lay the pattern on the leather and trace the outline with the scratch awl. You can also use a triangle ruler to mark the square.

STEP 2: Cut out the square. Use the ruler and utility knife to cut out the square.

STEP 3: Mark the stitch lines. Set the wing divider to ¼″ (0.5cm) and mark a stitch line on two adjacent sides of the square. Do not mark stitch lines on the remaining two sides.

STEP 4: Punch the stitch holes. Use the four-hole punch to punch the stitch lines you marked in the previous step. Remember to over-punch to keep your stitch holes straight.

STEP 5: Form the shape. Bring the punched edges of the square together with the stitch holes side-by-side, forming a cone. The top should be open, and the bottom should form a tip.

STEP 6: Measure the thread. Measure the stitch line on one side of the square and multiply by six to determine the length of thread you need. Cut the thread to length.

1A

1B

2

3

4A

4B

STEP 7: Thread the needle and begin stitching. Thread a needle onto each end of the cut thread. Working from the flesh side, push each needle through the bottom hole of each stitch line.

STEP 8: Stitch the project together. Cross-stitch the sides of the cone together. When finished stitching, tie the ends of the thread in a knot and secure it.

STEP 9: Punch the hanging hole. Punch a hole at the top of the cone to hang your project. Place your plant inside!

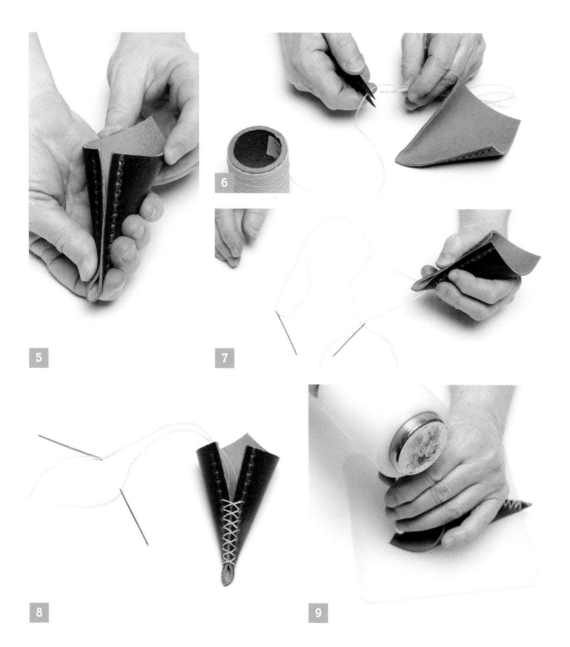

Tassel
Accessory Set

Get ready; it's time to tassel! Tassels have got to be one of the most popular leather accessories. I attach them to just about all of the bags that I make to sell. This section will show you how to make a beautiful tassel set, including earrings, a handbag tassel, and a key fob. While the tassel-making process is similar for each item, the sizes vary, and each one requires different hardware.

Cutting a Straight Line | pg. 18
Punching a Hole | pg. 20
Setting a Rivet | pg. 22

ESSENTIAL SKILLS

MATERIALS

- Leather: 7″ × 7″ (18 × 18cm), soft, 2–3oz
- Fishhook earring findings
- Jump rings
- Split ring
- ½″ (1cm) swivel hook

- Medium double-cap rivet
- Single-hole leather punch with ⁵⁄₃₂″ (4mm) tip
- Rivet setter and anvil
- Mallet
- Utility knife

- 2 rulers
- Poly cutting board
- Jewelry pliers
- Masking tape
- Contact cement
- Toothpick

TIP
This project requires making small and precise cuts, so, as always, be sure your knife is sharp and work slowly. Also, a set of small jewelry pliers may come in handy for the earrings.

Tassel Accessory Set

Tassel Earrings

STEP 1: Cut the leather. Measure and cut a 2″ × 1½″ (5 × 4cm) piece of leather with a utility knife. Then, cut the piece in half vertically so you have two 1″ × 1½″ (2.5 × 4cm) pieces.

STEP 2: Position and secure the first ruler. Place a ruler so it overlaps the short end of one strip by ½″ (1cm). Tape the ruler to your work surface to hold it in place.

STEP 3: Position the second ruler. Place the second ruler perpendicular to the first so it overlaps the long end of the strip by ⅛″ (0.5cm).

STEP 4: Cut the fringe. Use the utility knife to cut along the ruler positioned at the ⅛″ (1cm) mark to make the first fringe of the tassel. Work slowly and make multiple passes as needed. Cut to the bottom of the leather and then slide the ruler over another ⅛″ (0.5cm) and cut again. Continue this process to the end of the leather and then repeat with the remaining piece. Be sure to keep your utility knife straight (I have tilted it slightly for clarity in the photo).

STEP 5: Cut the tassel band. Measure and cut two 1″ × ¼″ (2.5 × 0.5cm) strips of leather with the utility knife.

1A

1B

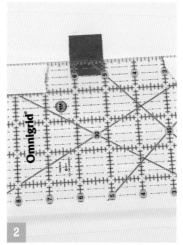

2

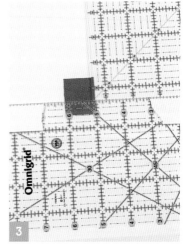

3

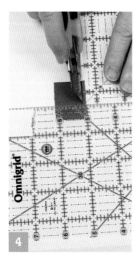

4

5A

5B

STEP 6: Thread the strip and glue it. Thread one of the strips through the jump ring until the ends are even. Put a dot of glue on the end of a toothpick and dab it onto the flesh side of the leather. (Follow all of the manufacturer's safety instructions for your chosen adhesive.) Fold the strip in half and squeeze until it stays in place.

STEP 7: Glue the fringed piece. Add more glue to the toothpick (if needed) and spread it on the uncut area of one fringed piece of leather on the flesh side.

STEP 8: Wrap the fringed piece around the strip. Wrap the fringed piece around the leather strip just below the jump ring as shown in the photo. Squeeze the pieces together until they stay in place.

STEP 9: Add the hook and repeat. Use jewelry pliers to open the jump ring and slide the earring hook onto it. Close the jump ring. Repeat Steps 6–9 with the remaining leather pieces to make the second earring.

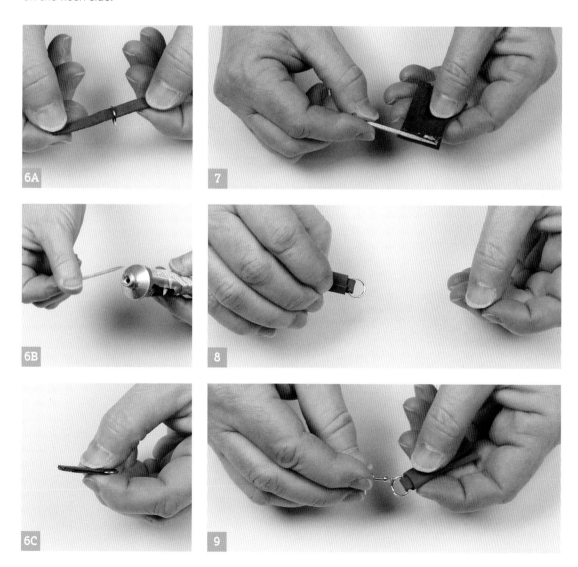

Tassel Accessory Set

Handbag Tassel

STEP 1: Cut the leather. Measure and cut a 5″ × 5″ (12.5 × 12.5cm) piece of leather with a utility knife. Place a ruler so it overlaps one edge of the leather by 1″ (2.5cm) and secure it with tape. Repeat Steps 3–4 from the earring project to cut the tassel fringe. Cut a 2″ × ½″ (2 × 1cm) piece of leather.

STEP 2: Add the glue. Add a thin strip of glue to the uncut area of the fringe piece on the flesh side.

STEP 3: Thread the strip and glue it. Thread the swivel hook onto the leather strip. Use a toothpick to apply glue to the ends of the strip on the flesh side. Fold the strip in half and squeeze the ends together until they stay in place.

STEP 4: Position the strip. Place the leather strip in the corner of the fringed piece as shown.

STEP 5: Roll and secure. Slowly begin rolling the fringed leather to wrap it around the smaller strip. Be sure to roll straight. When you come to the end, gently press on the roll until it stays in place.

STEP 6: Punch the rivet hole. Punch a hole at the top of the tassel for the rivet.

STEP 7: Set the rivet. Add the rivet to the tassel.

Key Fob

It's so easy to make a key fob tassel. Follow the instructions for the handbag tassel, but replace the swivel hook with a split ring!

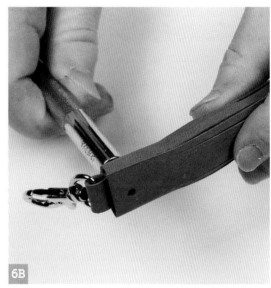

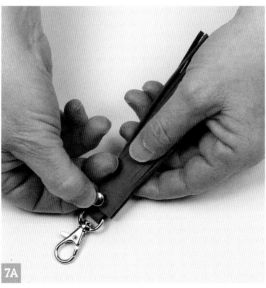

Terracotta Pot Wrap

Are you a plant parent? Do you love nurturing little plant babies and filling your house with containers in all shapes and sizes? Good, then you'll love this project! This rugged plant wrap is the perfect way to spruce up a standard terracotta pot. Here we will be making one sized to fit a miniature pot (perfect for a small cactus), but you can scale it up to fit whatever size you like. This project requires simple cross stitching, and I've used a blue thread to contrast with the brown leather. Have fun and get creative with your own color choices.

ESSENTIAL SKILLS

Cutting a Straight Line | pg. 18
Cutting a Curved Line | pg. 19
Using a Wing Divider | pg. 28
Using a Four-Hole Punch | pg. 29
How to Cross-Stitch | pg. 31

MATERIALS

- Leather: 3″ × 8″ (7.5 × 20.5cm), firm, 5oz
- Mini terracotta pot
- Four-hole leather punch
- Mallet
- Utility knife
- Leather scissors

- Scratch awl
- Ruler
- Poly cutting board
- Wing divider
- 2 blunt-end stitching needles

- Thread nipper
- Waxed thread
- Scissors
- Poster board
- Masking tape

TIP
Once you learn how to make a pattern using the tape method, you can make matching wraps for larger terracotta pots.

Terracotta Pot Wrap

STEP 1: Tape the pot. Masking tape is a perfect material to use when you want to measure round or uneven surfaces. Wrap it around your terracotta pot. Be sure to cover the entire pot thoroughly.

STEP 2: Remove the tape and trace the pattern. Slice a straight vertical line through the tape and remove it from the pot. Lay it on a piece of poster board (sticky side down) and trace it.

STEP 3: Cut the pattern. Use scissors to cut around the tape. When you have finished, gently remove the tape from the poster board to reveal the final pattern.

STEP 4: Trace the pattern onto the leather. Place the pattern on the leather and trace it with the scratch awl.

STEP 5: Cut the leather. Use the utiliy knife and ruler to cut along the straight lines and the leather scissors to cut along the curved lines. Be sure to cut slowly as you work your way around the curves.

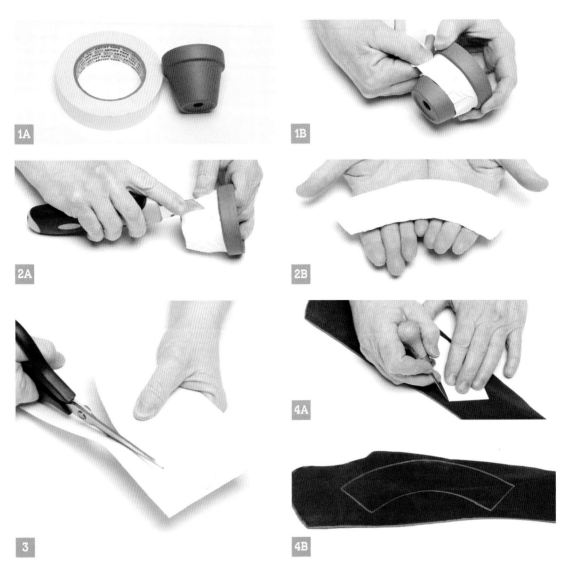

1A

1B

2A

2B

3

4A

4B

STEP 6: Mark the stitch lines. Set the wing divider to ¼″ (0.5cm) and mark a stitch line at each short end of the wrap.

STEP 7: Punch the stitch holes. Use the four-hole punch to punch the stitch lines on each end of the wrap. Remember to over-punch to keep your stitch holes straight.

STEP 8: Thread the needles and stitch. Measure the stitch line at one end of the wrap and multiply by six to determine the length of thread you need. Cut the thread to length and thread a needle onto each end. Bring the ends of the wrap together so the stitch holes are side-by-side. Cross-stitch the ends of the wrap together. Knot and secure the ends of the thread when finished.

STEP 9: Dress the pot and enjoy! Slide the wrap onto the terracotta pot and fill it with your favorite plant!

5

6

7

8

9

LEATHER CRAFT

Triangle Wallet

Who says beginner projects are boring? This clever little change purse is simple yet brilliantly designed. It's made from one piece of leather that elegantly folds up to hold (and protect) small valuables. And, because there is no sewing in this project, it literally goes together with a snap!

Cutting a Straight Line | pg. 18
Cutting a Curved Line | pg. 19
Punching a Hole | pg. 20
Setting a Snap | pg. 24

ESSENTIAL SKILLS

MATERIALS

- Leather: 4˝ × 11˝ (10 × 28cm), medium to firm, 3–4oz
- Two #20 snaps
- Single-hole leather punch with ⁵⁄₃₂˝ (4mm) tip

- Snap setter and anvil
- Mallet
- Utility knife
- Leather scissors

- Scratch awl
- Ruler
- Poly cutting board
- Triangle Wallet Pattern (page 123)

TIP
This smart wallet has no front or back.
You can open it from either side!

Triangle Wallet

STEP 1: Trace the pattern. Lay the pattern on the leather and trace the outline with the scratch awl.

STEP 2: Mark the snap holes. Use the scratch awl to mark the holes for the snaps on the leather.

STEP 3: Cut the pattern piece. Use the utility knife to cut along the straight lines marked on the leather. Use leather scissors to cut along the curved lines. You can cut the curves very carefully using the utility knife if you do not have leather scissors.

STEP 4: Punch the snap holes. Punch the holes for the snaps.

STEP 5: Set the snap tops. Set the snap tops in the outer holes of the wallet. The caps should be on the grain side of the leather.

STEP 6: Set the snap bottoms. Set the snap bottoms in the inner holes of the wallet. The posts should be on the flesh side of the leather.

STEP 7: Make the first fold. Hold the project horizontally, with the flesh side of the leather facing up. Fold the wallet in half on a diagonal with flesh sides facing so the ends are perpendicular as shown.

STEP 8: Finish folding. Fold one end of the wallet over and snap it in place. Flip the wallet over and repeat with the other end.

1

2

3A

3B

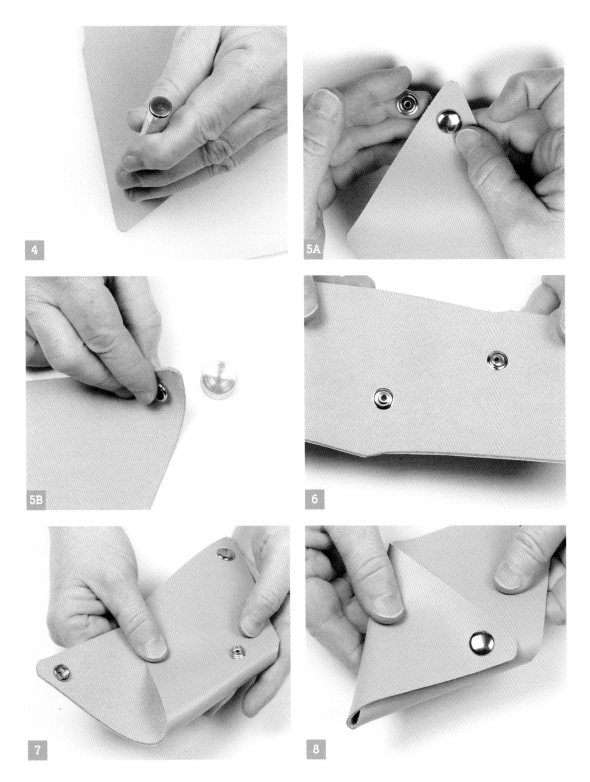

Trinket Tray

This trinket tray will be your new go-to for daily necessities, whether you place it on your bedside table, nightstand, or desk. It's perfectly sized to fit a cell phone, earbuds, loose change, and any other small items that come out of your pocket before bed! This project gets its structure by using heavyweight leather and joining the corners with rivets. As a result, it's a durable accessory that's practical and beautiful.

Cutting a Straight Line | pg. 18
Punching a Hole | pg. 20
Setting a Rivet | pg. 22

ESSENTIAL SKILLS

MATERIALS

- Leather: 8˝ × 8˝ (20.5 × 20.5cm), firm, 5oz
- 4 medium double-cap rivets in antique gold
- Single-hole leather punch with ⁵⁄₃₂˝ (4mm) tip
- Rivet setter and anvil
- Mallet
- Utility knife
- Scratch awl
- Ruler
- Poly cutting board
- Trinket Tray Pattern (page 124)

TIP
When purchasing a mixed bag of rivets, match the posts and caps before starting a new project.

Trinket Tray

STEP 1: Trace the pattern. Lay the pattern on the leather and trace the outline with the scratch awl.

STEP 2: Mark the holes. Use the scratch awl to mark the holes for the rivets on the leather (two in each corner).

STEP 3: Cut the leather square. Use the utility knife and ruler to cut out the square. Be sure your blade is sharp!

STEP 4: Punch the holes. Punch the holes for the rivets.

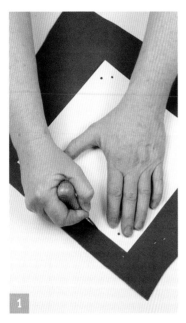

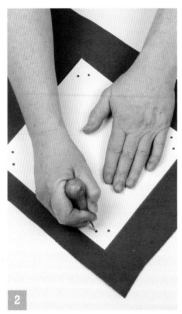

STEP 5: Add the rivet. Squeeze one corner of the square together with grain sides facing so the two rivet holes line up. Push a rivet post through the holes from the flesh side. Snap the rivet cap in place on the post.

STEP 6: Set the rivets. Finish setting the rivet. Repeat with the remaining corners of the tray.

STEP 7: Shape the tray. Use your hands to mold the trinket tray until you are happy with the shape.

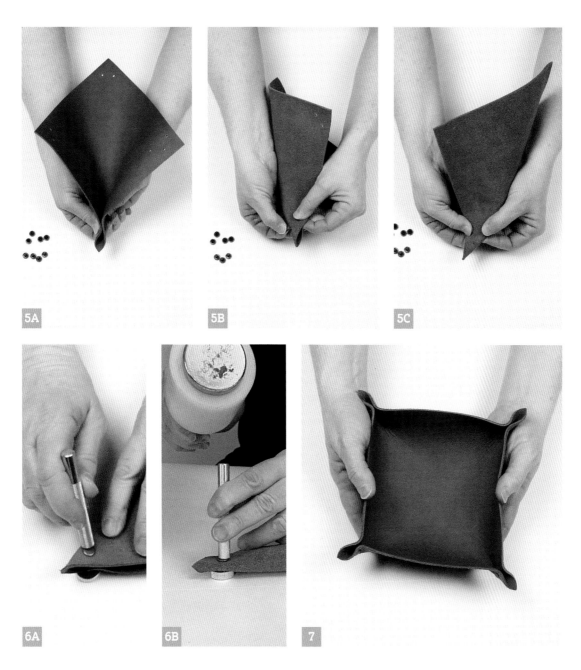

5A

5B

5C

6A

6B

7

LEATHER CRAFT

Vase Wrap

Flowers are always a good idea, especially when arranged in
a gorgeous leather-wrapped vase! This project will teach you how
to transform an ordinary cylindrical glass vase into a handsome
statement piece with simple leathercraft techniques and
beautiful hand stitching. If you have a vase the same size as
I am using, skip the first step and start at the second.

Cutting a Straight Line | pg. 18
Using a Wing Divider | pg. 28
Using a Four-Hole Punch | pg. 29
How to Cross-Stitch | pg. 31

ESSENTIAL SKILLS

MATERIALS

- Leather: 12″ × 7″ (30.5 × 18cm), firm, 5oz
- Cylindrical glass vase: 7½″ tall, 10¾″ circumference (19cm tall, 27.5cm circumference)
- Four-hole leather punch
- Mallet

- Utility knife
- Scratch awl
- Ruler
- Poly cutting board
- Wing divider
- 2 blunt-end stitching needles

- Thread nipper
- Waxed thread
- Tape measure
- Vase Wrap Pattern (page 125)

TIP
*Want to create beautiful leather wraps
for vases in other sizes? No problem!
Follow the instructions in the first step
to make a custom pattern.*

Vase Wrap

STEP 1: Measure the vase (if you are not using the pattern provided). Measure the vase's circumference and add ½″ (1cm) to determine the width of the pattern. Then measure the height of the vase and subtract approximately ¼″ (0.5cm) to determine the height. Plot these measurements on a piece of poster board to create your pattern.

STEP 2: Mark and cut the pattern. Lay the pattern on the leather and trace the outline with the scratch awl. Then cut out the piece using the utility knife and ruler.

STEP 3: Mark the stitch line. Set the wing divider to ¼″ (0.5cm) and mark a stitch line at each short end of the wrap.

STEP 4: Punch the stitch holes. Use the four-hole punch to punch the stitch lines on each end of the wrap. Remember to over-punch to keep your stitch holes straight.

STEP 5: Determine thread length and cross-stitch. Measure the stitch line at one side of the wrap and multiply by six to determine the length of thread you need. Cut the thread to length and thread a needle onto each end. Bring the ends of the wrap together so the stitch holes are side-by-side. Cross-stitch the ends of the wrap together. Knot and secure the ends of the thread when finished.

STEP 6: Insert vase and fill with flowers. Slide the leather wrap onto the vase. Add a bouquet for the finishing touch!

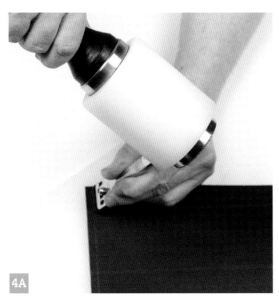

4A

4B

5A

5B

6

Wall Pocket

Are you ready to move up to a larger project? Great! Here we will make a beautiful wall pocket perfect for organizing mail, magazines, and important documents. Or, if you want to get creative, you can use it to display beautiful faux flowers. This project is made with a heavyweight leather and saddle stitched to give it style and structure. Be sure to refer to the pattern in the back of the book if you need help finding the fold lines.

Cutting a Straight Line | pg. 18
Cutting a Curved Line | pg. 19
Punching a Hole | pg. 20
Using a Wing Divider | pg. 28
Using a Four-Hole Punch | pg. 29
How to Saddle Stitch | pg. 34

ESSENTIAL SKILLS

MATERIALS

- Leather: 24″ × 24″ (61 × 61cm), firm, 5–6 oz
- Single-hole leather punch with 5/32″ (4mm) tip
- Four-hole leather punch
- Mallet

- Utility knife
- Leather scissors
- Scratch awl
- Ruler
- Poly cutting board
- Wing divider

- 2 blunt-end stitching needles
- Thread nipper
- Waxed thread
- Sandpaper (optional)
- Wall Pocket Pattern (page 126)

TIP
Use an upholstery tack to hang your wall pocket.
You can find them at most craft or quilt shops.

Wall Pocket

STEP 1: Trace the pattern. Lay the pattern on the leather and trace the outline and mark the hanging hole with the scratch awl.

STEP 2: Cut the pattern. Use the utility knife to cut along the straight lines marked on the leather. Go slowly and turn the ruler to guide your cuts as you move around the pattern. Use leather scissors to cut along the curved lines.

STEP 3: Sand if needed. Smooth out any bumps on the rounded corners with sandpaper.

STEP 4: Mark the stitch lines. Set the wing divider to ¼" (0.5cm) and mark the stitch lines along the edges of the flaps following the pattern. The photo below shows how the piece will look when the flaps are folded and the stitch lines are joined.

STEP 5: Punch the stitch holes. Use the four-hole punch to punch the stitch lines you marked in the previous step. You should have room to punch 24 holes along each stitch line. Remember to over-punch to keep your stitch holes straight.

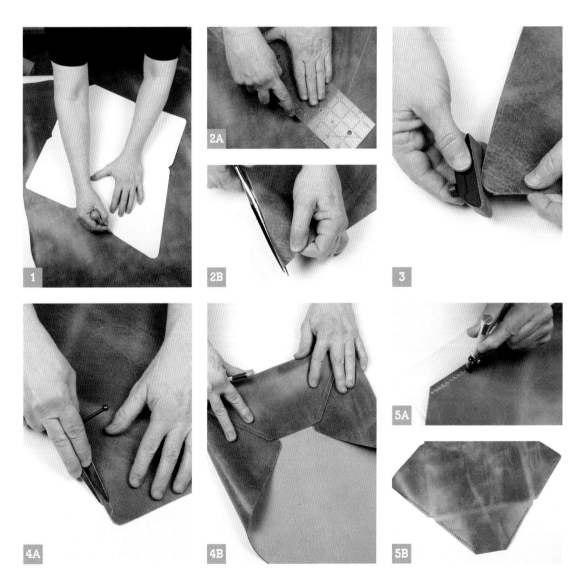

STEP 6: Begin stitching. Cut a 24″ (61cm)-long piece of thread and thread a needle onto each end. Fold one of the side flaps in, then fold the bottom flap up over it so the stitch holes align. Starting in the bottom corner, begin saddle stitching the two pieces together.

STEP 7: Finishing stitching the first flap. Continue saddle stitching until you reach the end of the stitch holes. Backstitch through three holes to secure the stitching, and then remove your needles and snip the thread.

STEP 8: Stitch the second flap. Repeat Steps 6–7 to stitch the remaining side flap to the bottom flap.

STEP 9: Punch the hanging hole. Punch a hanging hole at the top of the pocket where marked. Your wall pocket is complete!

6

7

8A

8B

8C

10

Wrap Bracelet

Here is a simple yet stunning leather jewelry project that you can make in an afternoon. It can be sized to fit any wrist and is surprisingly comfortable to wear. I am showing it in soft brown leather with an antique brass O-ring, but it would also look just as beautiful in black leather with silver hardware. Get creative and use materials that match your style.

Cutting a Straight Line | pg. 18
Punching a Hole | pg. 20
Setting a Rivet | pg. 22
Setting a Button Stud | pg. 26

ESSENTIAL SKILLS

MATERIALS

- Leather: ½″ × 24″ (1 × 61cm), soft to medium, 3oz
- Small button stud in antique brass
- O-ring in antique brass

- 2 medium double-cap rivets in antique brass
- Single-hole leather punch with ⁵⁄₃₂″ (4mm) tip
- #4 button hole punch
- Rivet setter and anvil

- Mallet
- Utility knife
- Leather scissors
- Ruler
- Poly cutting board

TIP
Try rounding the ends of this bracelet
for a more finished look.

Wrap Bracelet

STEP 1: Cut a strip. Use the utility knife and ruler to cut a 24″ × ½″ (61 × 1cm) strip of leather.

STEP 2: Mark the cut line. Lay the strip against the ruler and mark the center point at 12″ (30.5cm).

STEP 3: Cut the strip. Use the leather scissors to cut the strip in half at the center point.

STEP 4: Thread the first end. Thread 1″ (2.5cm) of one of the leather strips through the O-ring

and fold it over the ring so the flesh sides are facing.

STEP 5: Punch the rivet hole. Punch a hole in the center of the folded end of the strip, punching through both layers.

STEP 6: Set the rivet and repeat on the other side. Set the rivet in the hole you created in the previous step. Repeat Steps 4–6 to attach the remaining leather strip to the other side of the O-ring.

STEP 7: Measure and punch the button stud hole. Use the ruler to measure and mark ½″ (1cm) in from the end of one strip. Punch a hole where marked.

STEP 8: Insert the button stud. Set the button stud in the hole you created in the previous step.

STEP 9: Punch the closure hole. Use the ruler to measure and mark ½″ (1cm) in from the end of the other strip (the one without the button stud). Punch a button hole where marked. If desired, you can punch a second button hole ½″ (1cm) away from the first one so you have sizing options.

STEP 10: Wrap and close. Wrap the bracelet around your wrist so that the O-ring is in the center and the closure is in the back. Photo 10B shows the two holes that can be used to adjust the size of the bracelet.

Wristlet

A wristlet is a classic design and the perfect accessory. It's big enough to fit your essentials and compact enough for easy travel. You can use this handy bag with the wrist strap or leave the strap off to use it as a clutch. This project includes more steps than some of the others, so for that reason, we will break it down into three parts. Take your time and work slowly. This is a bag that will never go out of fashion!

Cutting a Straight Line | pg. 18
Cutting a Curved Line | pg. 19
Punching a Hole | pg. 20
Setting a Rivet | pg. 22
Setting a Snap | pg. 24
Using a Wing Divider | pg. 28
Using a Four-Hole Punch | pg. 29
How to Saddle Stitch | pg. 34

ESSENTIAL SKILLS

MATERIALS

- Leather: 12″ × 15″ (30.5 × 38cm), medium, 4–5 oz
- ¾″ (2cm) clasp
- ¾″ (2cm) D-ring
- Medium double-cap rivet
- #20 snap
- Single-hole leather punch with ⁵⁄₃₂″ (4mm) tip
- Four-hole leather punch
- ¾″ (2cm) rounded strap end punch

- Rivet setter and anvil
- Snap setter and anvil
- Mallet
- Utility knife
- Leather scissors
- Scratch awl
- Ruler
- Poly cutting board

- Wing divider
- 2 blunt-end stitching needles
- Thread nipper
- Waxed thread
- Sandpaper (optional)
- Thin, double-sided tape
- Wristlet Pattern (page 127)

TIP
The strap can go on either side, so think about your preference and work accordingly.

Wristlet

Preparing the Body Parts

STEP 1: Trace the pattern. Lay the pattern on the leather and trace the outline with the scratch awl.

STEP 2: Cut the pattern pieces. Use the utility knife and ruler to cut along the straight lines marked on the leather. Use the leather scissors to cut along the curved lines.

STEP 3: Sand if needed. Lightly sand the corners and any other edges that need to be smoothed.

STEP 4: Mark the snap holes. Place the pattern over the leather cutout. Mark the position of the snap holes with the scratch awl.

STEP 5: Punch the snap holes. Punch the holes marked for the snaps.

STEP 6: Set the snap. Set the snap. Be sure to position the pieces so the snap will close when the wristlet is assembled.

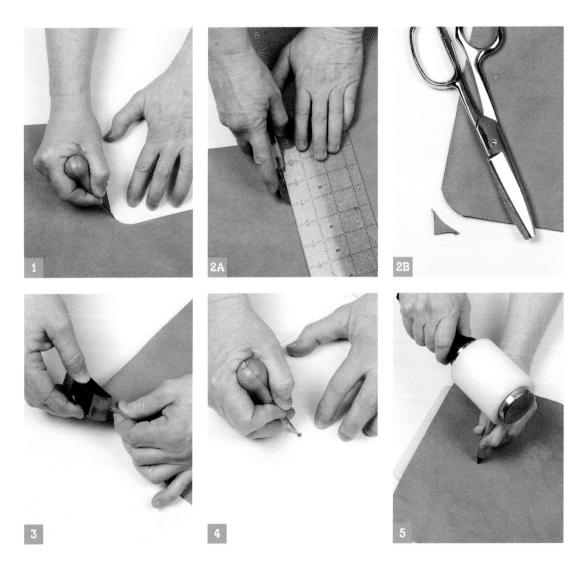

STEP 7: Tape the sides. On the flesh side of the leather, attach a piece of tape to the wristlet going from the bottom edge to about 9½″ (24cm) up the side. Repeat on the other side. Remove the backing from the tape.

STEP 8: Fold and pinch. Fold the bottom edge of the leather up to the 9½″ (24cm) line. The flesh sides should be facing. Press the layers together so the fold is held in place by the tape.

STEP 9: Cut D-ring strap. Cut a ¾″ × 2½″ (2 × 6.5cm) strip of leather.

STEP 10: Add the D-ring. Thread the leather strip through the D-ring. Add a strip of double-sided tape to each end of the strip on the flesh side.

STEP 11: Secure the ends. Remove the backing from the tape and fold the leather strip so the ends come together, flesh sides facing. Now add a piece of double-sided tape to the end of the strip on the top and bottom.

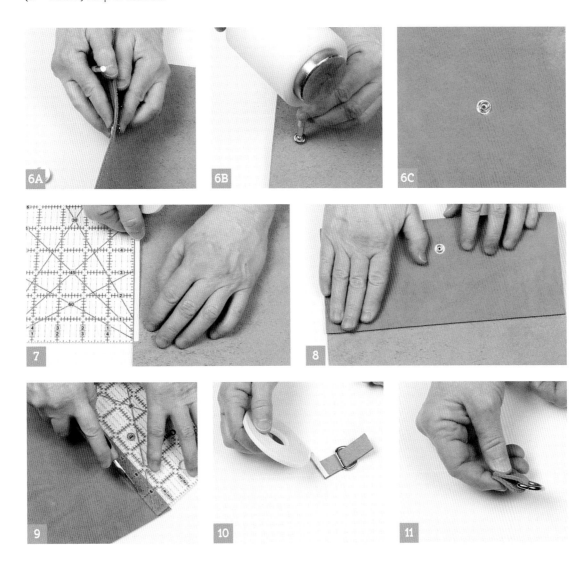

Wristlet

Stitching the Sides

STEP 1: Position the D-ring strap. Position the D-ring and strap about ½˝ (1cm) from the top of the wristlet pocket.

STEP 2: Insert the D-ring strap. Remove the backing from the double-sided tape. Place the strap between the layers of the wristlet pocket. Squeeze the layers together to hold the strap in place.

STEP 3: Mark the stitch line. Set the wing divider to ¼˝ (0.5cm) and mark a stitch line on each side of the wristlet. Work slowly and precisely as straight lines are critical for stitching this project.

STEP 4: Punch the stitch holes. Use the four-hole punch to punch the stitch lines on each side of the wristlet. Remember to over-punch and hold the punch straight up and down to keep your stitch holes neat.

STEP 5: Start stitching strap side. Cut a 21˝ (53.5cm)-long piece of thread. Starting at one corner of the wristlet, begin saddle stitching the side of the wristlet.

STEP 6: Complete stitching. Continue stitching until you reach the end of the stitch holes. Backstitch through three holes to reinforce the stitches. Snip the thread and tuck the loose ends into one of the stitch holes to conceal them. Repeat Steps 5–6 to stitch the other side of the wristlet.

Preparing and Attaching the Strap

STEP 1: Cut the wristlet strap. Cut a ¾″ × 15″ (2 × 38cm) piece of leather.

STEP 2: Round the edges. This step is optional but will give your project a finished look if you choose to do it. Use a ¾″ (2cm) rounded strap end punch or a pair of leather scissors to punch or cut the ends of the strip so they are rounded.

STEP 3: Thread the wrist strap. Thread 1″ (2.5cm) of the strip through the clasp and fold it over so the flesh sides are facing. Bring the other end of the strip up and place it on top of the first end, creating three layers of leather.

STEP 4: Set the rivet. Punch a hole in the center of the layered end of the strip, punching through all three layers. Set a rivet in the hole.

STEP 5: Attach the strap. Attach the clasp to the D-ring and your project is complete!

Appendix

In the coming pages, you will find patterns for all projects requiring them in this book. I recommend that you photocopy the patterns (or print them using the download link provided on page 116) and trace them onto poster board to create a set of reusable templates. Then, use the scratch awl to trace the patterns and mark holes onto your leather.

The solid outline on the patterns represents the trim. The dotted lines represent the hole punches for stitching, and the dashed lines represent folds. Singular solid dots represent holes for snaps or rivets.

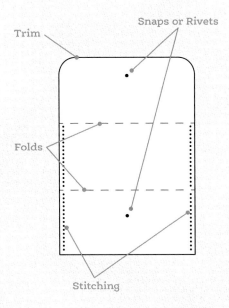

Patterns

Downloadable Patterns

You can download and print the full-sized patterns for these leathercraft projects at:

tinyurl.com/11491-patterns-download

Accessing and Using Patterns

To access the patterns through the tiny url, type the web address provided into your browser window.

Print directly from the browser window or download the pattern.

- **To print at home**, print the letter-size pages, selecting 100% size on the printer. Use dashed/dotted lines to trim, layer, and tape together pages as needed.

- **To print at a copyshop**, save the full-size pages to a thumb drive or email them to your local copyshop for printing.

Artist Roll,
instructions on *page 38*

MAIN BODY

Enlarge Pattern 263%

Artist Roll

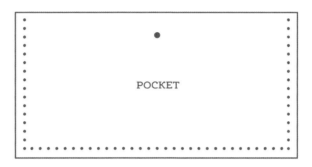

POCKET

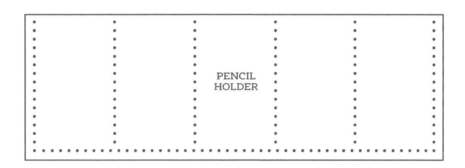

PENCIL HOLDER

POCKET FLAP

TOP FLAP

Enlarge Patterns 263%

Patterns

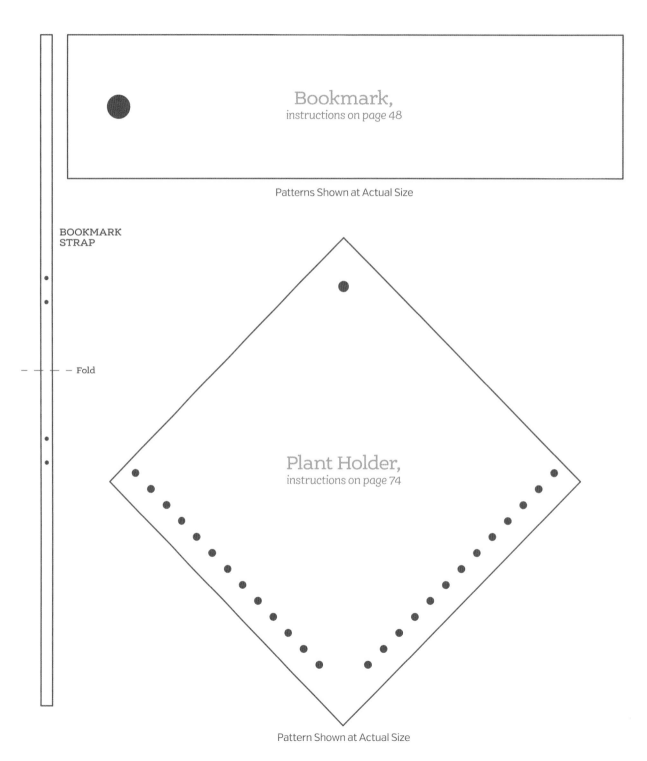

Bookmark,
instructions on page 48

Patterns Shown at Actual Size

BOOKMARK
STRAP

— Fold

Plant Holder,
instructions on page 74

Pattern Shown at Actual Size

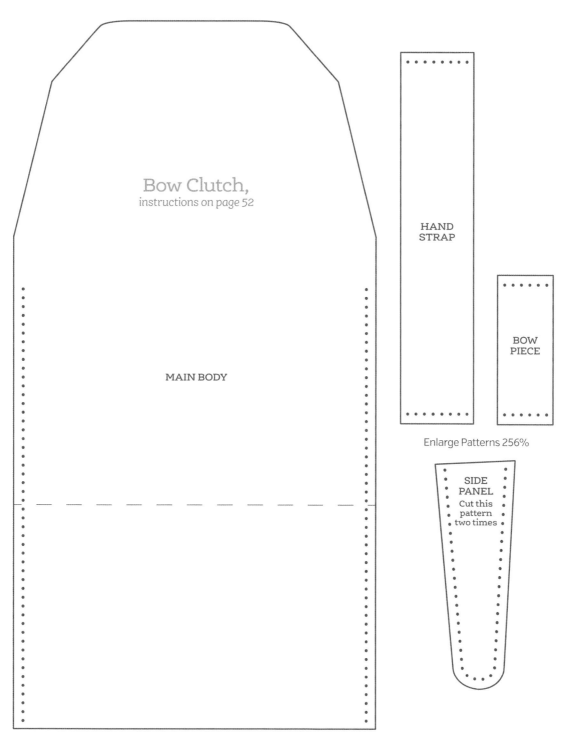

Bow Clutch,
instructions on page 52

MAIN BODY

HAND STRAP

BOW PIECE

Enlarge Patterns 256%

SIDE PANEL
Cut this pattern two times

Enlarge Pattern 256%

Patterns

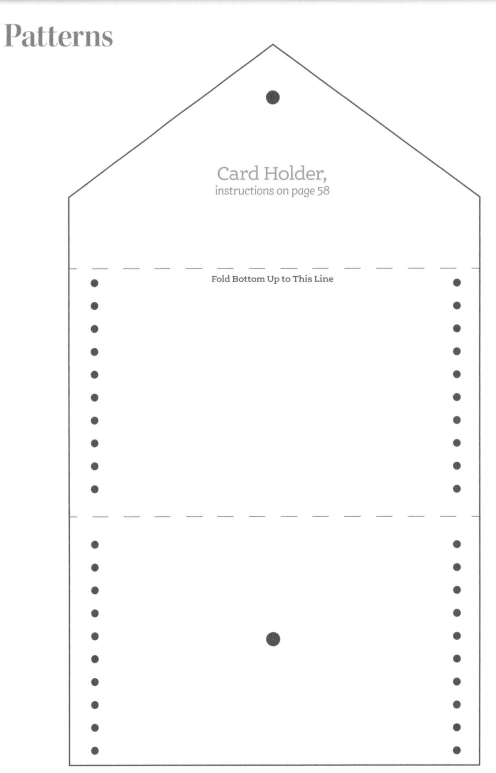

Card Holder,
instructions on page 58

Fold Bottom Up to This Line

Pattern Shown at Actual Size

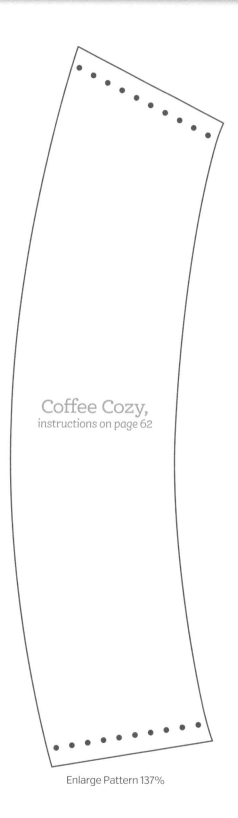

Coffee Cozy,
instructions on page 62

Enlarge Pattern 137%

Patterns

Cord Keeper,
instructions on page 66

Pattern Shown at Actual Size

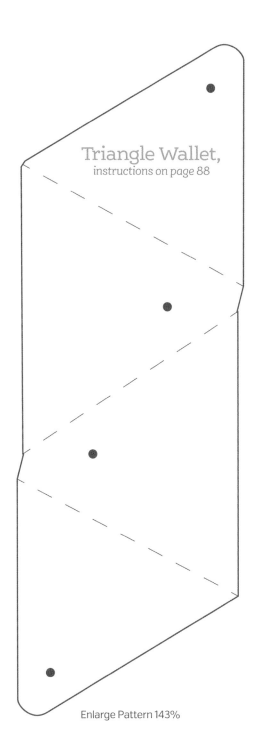

Triangle Wallet,
instructions on *page 88*

Enlarge Pattern 143%

Patterns

Trinket Tray,
instructions on page 92

Enlarge Pattern 133%

Vase Wrap,
instructions on page 96

Enlarge Pattern 154%

Patterns

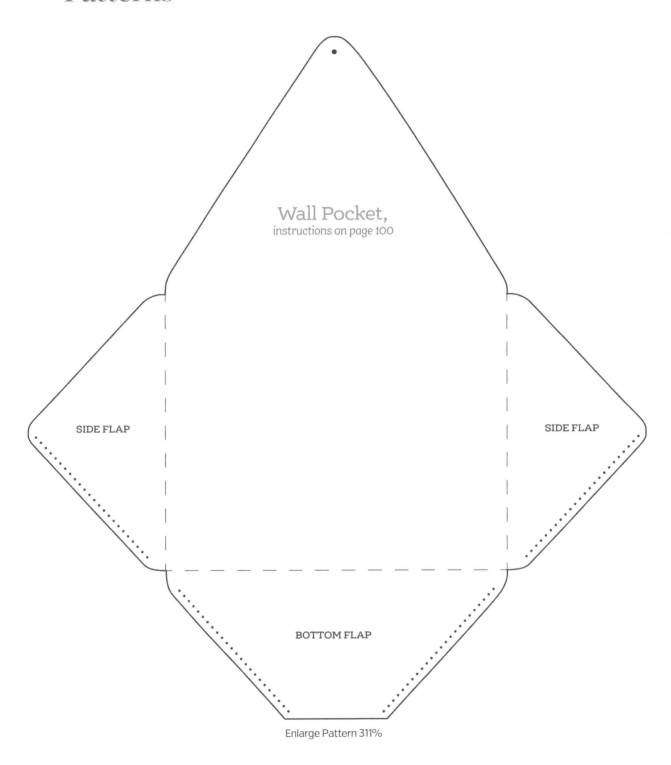

Wall Pocket,
instructions on page 100

SIDE FLAP

SIDE FLAP

BOTTOM FLAP

Enlarge Pattern 311%

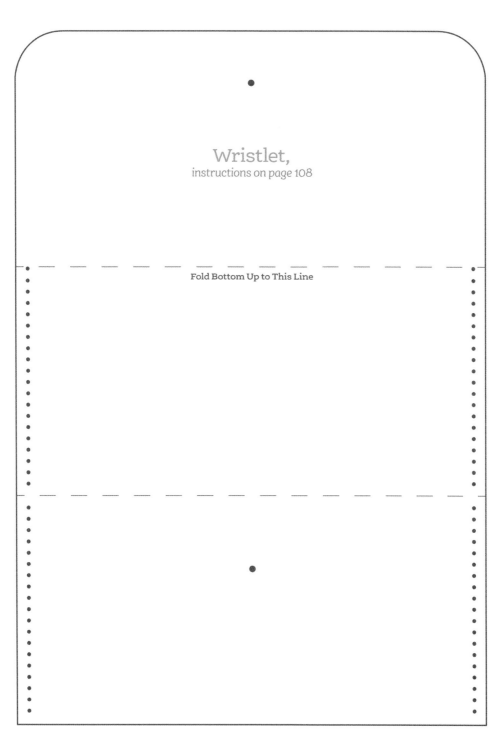

Wristlet,
instructions on page 108

Fold Bottom Up to This Line

Enlarge Pattern 200%